Charles Hallé

Charles Hallé's Practical Pianoforte School

Sonata in A Flat

Charles Hallé

Charles Hallé's Practical Pianoforte School
Sonata in A Flat

ISBN/EAN: 9783744783705

Printed in Europe, USA, Canada, Australia, Japan

Cover: Foto ©Thomas Meinert / pixelio.de

More available books at **www.hansebooks.com**

SECTION V. Nº 1.

CHARLES HALLÉ'S
PRACTICAL
Pianoforte School.

SONATA
IN A FLAT,
OP. 110.
BY
L. VAN BEETHOVEN.

ENT STA HALL

PRICE 6s/=

FORSYTH BROTHERS,
272ª Regent Circus, Oxford Street, London
Cross Street and South King Street, Manchester.

PREFACE.

A few remarks will suffice to explain the object of this Publication and its distinguishing features.

"THE PRACTICAL PIANOFORTE SCHOOL" will consist of a series of Pieces selected from the best Composers, and calculated to guide students, by gradual steps, from the very beginning to the highest degree of execution, and at the same time to form their taste and style.

The Work will be divided into five sections, namely, ELEMENTARY, EASY, MODERATELY DIFFICULT, DIFFICULT, and VERY DIFFICULT. Commencing with the rudiments of Musical Notation, the Pieces will succeed each other in such progressive order that Students, after having mastered one number, may safely proceed to the next, thus sparing both Teacher and Pupil the difficult task of selection.

Each Piece will be prefaced by a certain number of Exercises written expressly by me for this Publication, and having some bearing upon the difficulties of the Composition which they introduce. The daily practice of these Exercises should always precede that of the piece, until both are completely mastered.

Long experience has convinced me that the usual mode of fingering is insufficient to guard Pupils from the danger of contracting bad habits, as they cannot always be under the eye of the Master, and yet require a *constant* guide in this more than in any other matter. *Every note therefore will be fingered*, except that in the case of reiterated chords the fingering will be marked only once, and Octaves will not be fingered when they are to be played with the thumb and fourth finger.

All *Turns, Shakes, Appoggiaturas*, and other Ornaments, will be clearly explained in foot-notes, whenever their proper execution may be doubtful; and in the more advanced pieces there will be found, in brackets, *supplementary signs of expression*, where they may appear to me to facilitate the correct rendering of the Composer's intention. These I give on my own responsibility, and as my interpretation of the master-pieces which I have made my study for many years.

Two Metronome marks will be prefixed to every Piece and Exercise;—the first indicating the time beyond which Students ought not to venture before they can play both Piece and Exercise without fault; and the second giving the correct time.

The utmost endeavours will be used to keep the entire Work free from errors, and the greatest care bestowed upon its publication, which the long and intimate relations I have had with Messrs FORSYTH BROTHERS have led me to entrust to them.

A long experience as a Teacher and Performer, and a thorough acquaintance with the whole range of Pianoforte Music, encourage me in the hope that this "Practical Pianoforte School" may prove what I wish it to be—a safe guide towards a sound Musical Education.

CHARLES HALLÉ.

SONATA.

In A flat major.

L. van BEETHOVEN, Op. 110.

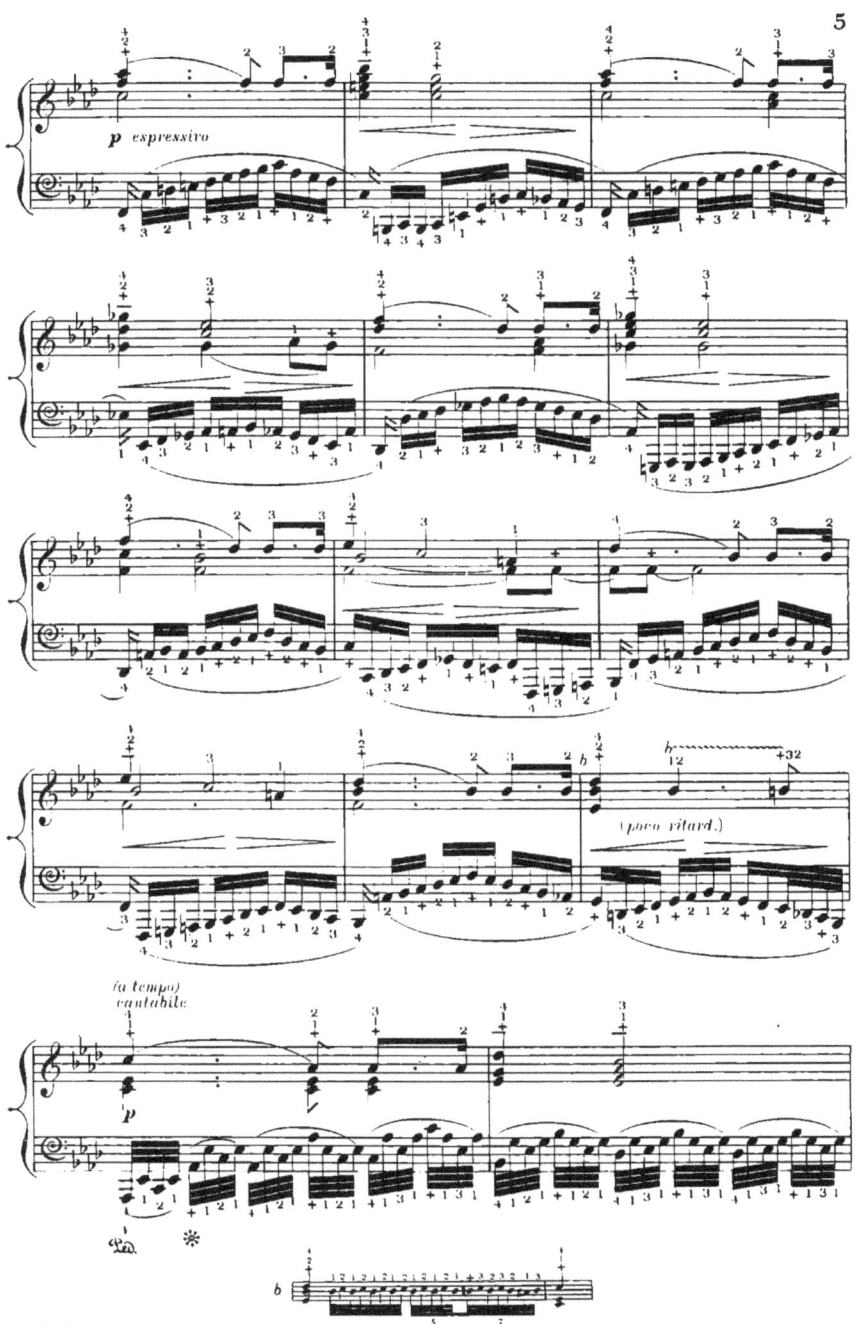

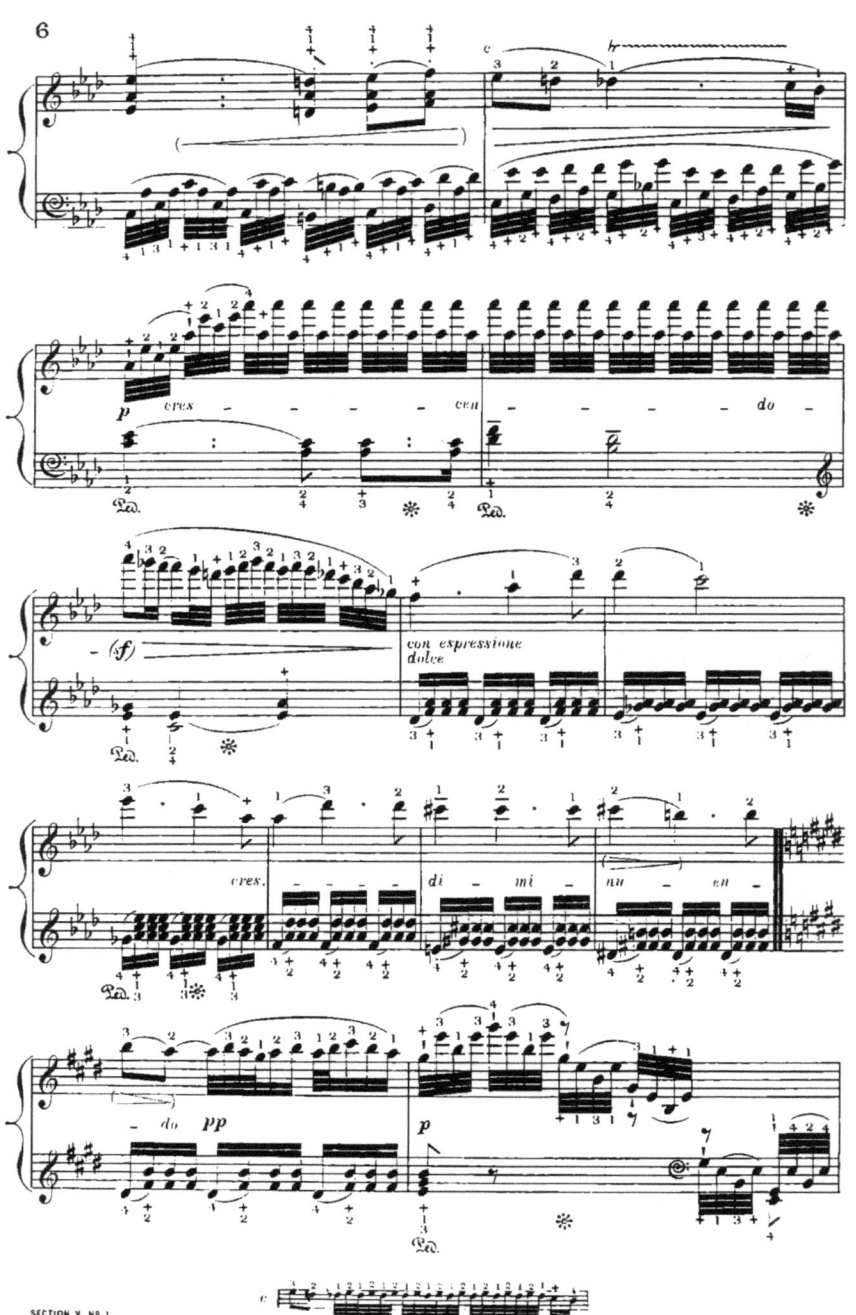

e) *The second note, played with the second finger, is to be sounded softly (not tied to the first.)*
SECTION V. N° 1.

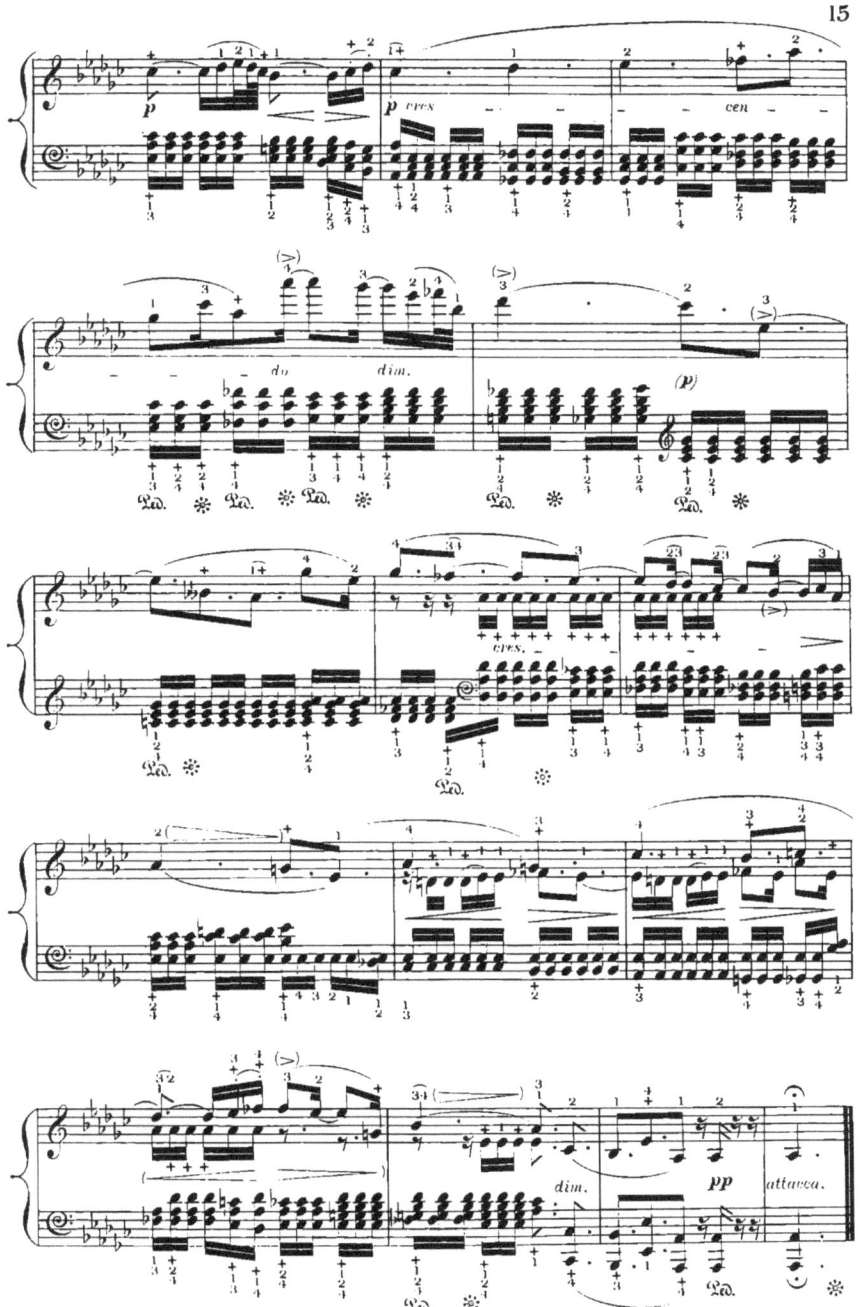

M. M. (♩. = 54.) (♩. = 58.)
L'istesso tempo di arioso.
p
cres.
dim.
p
dim.
cres.
dim.
p
poco cres
cen
do
(p)
pp

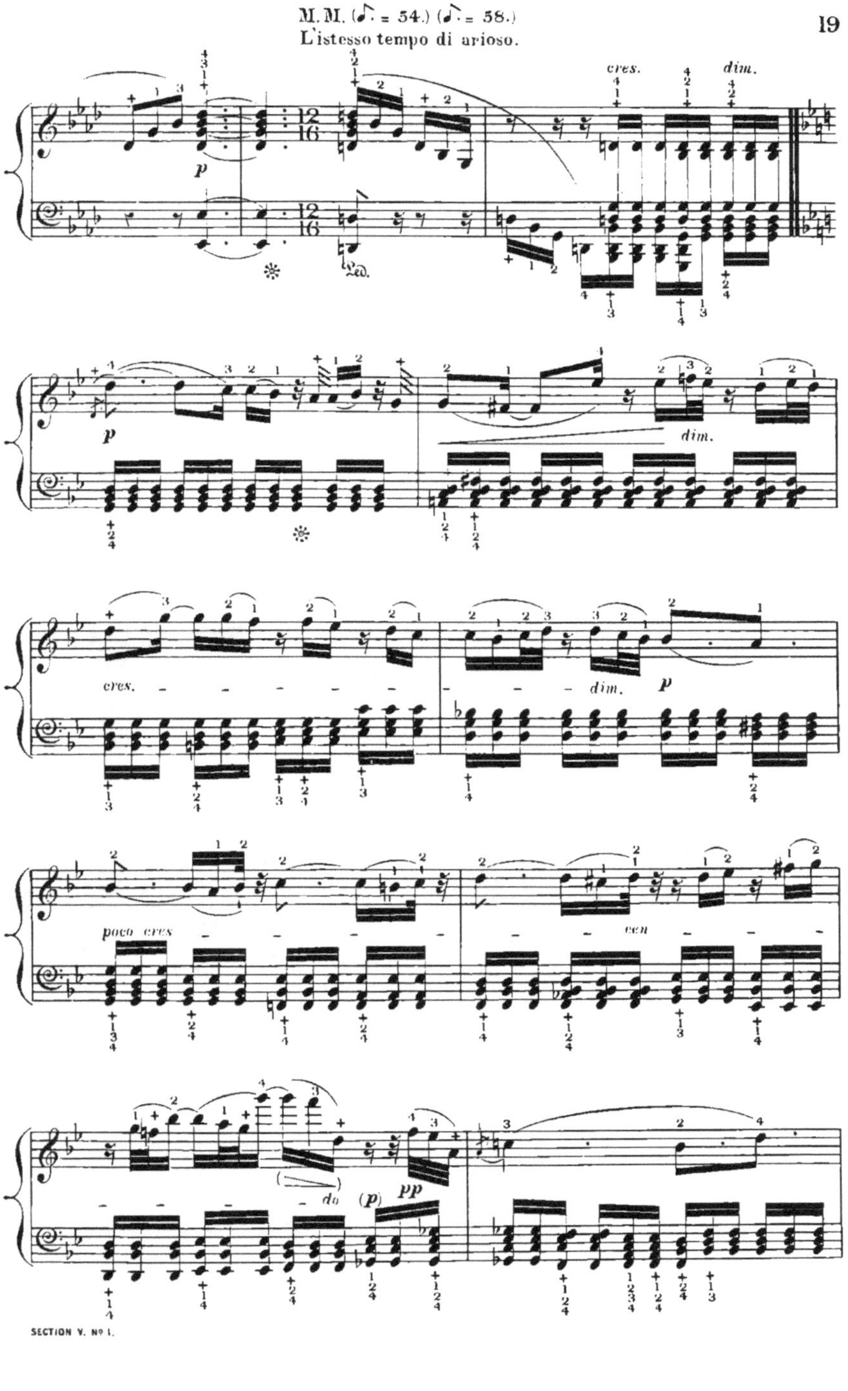

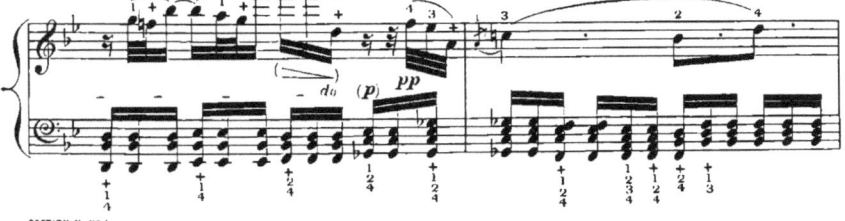

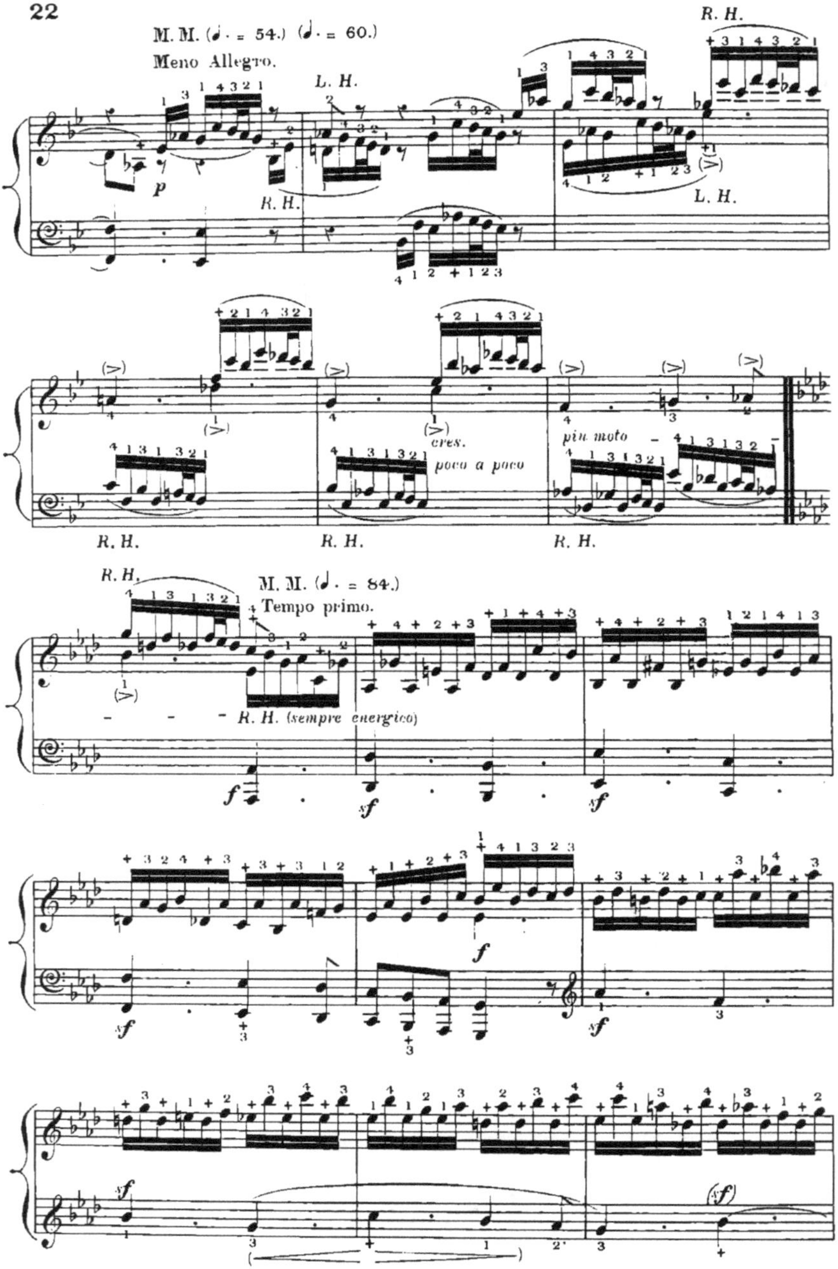

22

SECTION V. N° 1.

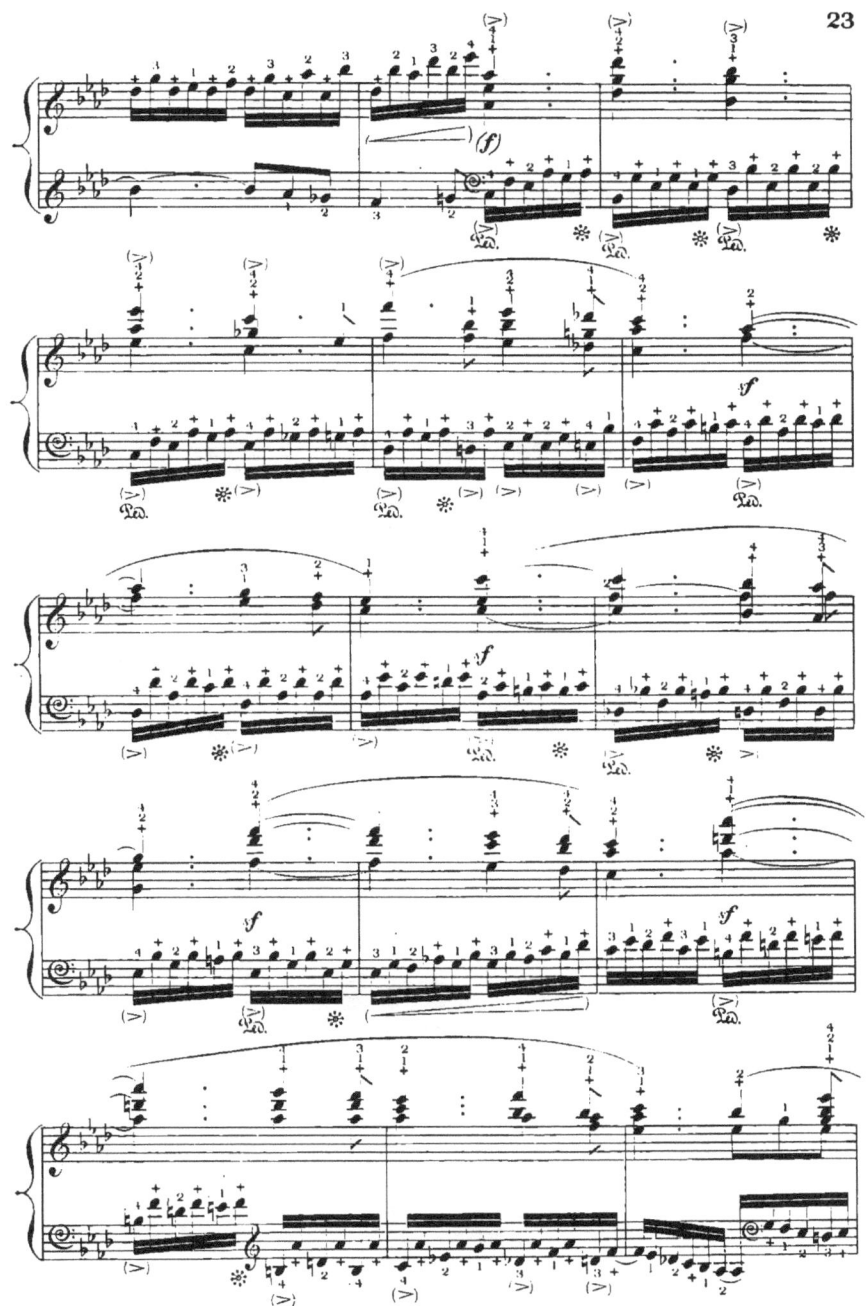

CHARLES HALLÉ'S
PRACTICAL
Pianoforte School.

TWO
PHANTASIE-STÜCKE
from Op. 12.
BY
ROBERT SCHUMANN.

ENT. STA. HALL.   PRICE 4/6

FORSYTH BROTHERS.
272.ª Regent Circus, Oxford Street, London,
AND
Cross Street and South King Street, Manchester.

PREFACE.

A few remarks will suffice to explain the object of this Publication and its distinguishing features.

"THE PRACTICAL PIANOFORTE SCHOOL" will consist of a series of Pieces selected from the best Composers, and calculated to guide students, by gradual steps, from the very beginning to the highest degree of execution, and at the same time to form their taste and style.

The Work will be divided into five sections, namely, ELEMENTARY, EASY, MODERATELY DIFFICULT, DIFFICULT, and VERY DIFFICULT. Commencing with the rudiments of Musical Notation, the Pieces will succeed each other in such progressive order that Students, after having mastered one number, may safely proceed to the next, thus sparing both Teacher and Pupil the difficult task of selection.

Each Piece will be prefaced by a certain number of Exercises written expressly by me for this Publication, and having some bearing upon the difficulties of the Composition which they introduce. The daily practice of these Exercises should always precede that of the piece, until both are completely mastered.

Long experience has convinced me that the usual mode of fingering is insufficient to guard Pupils from the danger of contracting bad habits, as they cannot always be under the eye of the Master, and yet require a *constant* guide in this more than in any other matter. *Every note therefore will be fingered*, except that in the case of reiterated chords the fingering will be marked only once, and Octaves will not be fingered when they are to be played with the thumb and fourth finger.

All *Turns*, *Shakes*, *Appoggiaturas*, and other Ornaments, will be clearly explained in foot-notes, whenever their proper execution may be doubtful; and in the more advanced pieces there will be found, in brackets, *supplementary signs of expression*, where they may appear to me to facilitate the correct rendering of the Composer's intention. These I give on my own responsibility, and as my interpretation of the master-pieces which I have made my study for many years.

Two Metronome marks will be prefixed to every Piece and Exercise;—the first indicating the time beyond which Students ought not to venture before they can play both Piece and Exercise without fault; and the second giving the correct time.

The utmost endeavours will be used to keep the entire Work free from errors, and the greatest care bestowed upon its publication, which the long and intimate relations I have had with Messrs FORSYTH BROTHERS have led me to entrust to them.

A long experience as a Teacher and Performer, and a thorough acquaintance with the whole range of Pianoforte Music, encourage me in the hope that this "Practical Pianoforte School" may prove what I wish it to be—a safe guide towards a sound Musical Education.

CHARLES HALLÉ.

DAILY EXERCISES.

Each repeat to be played ten times without stopping.

"WARUM?"

R. SCHUMANN Op. 12, No. 3.

"TRAUMES — WIRREN."

R. SCHUMANN Op. 12, No 7.

SECTION V. N°.3.

CHARLES HALLÉ'S
PRACTICAL
Pianoforte School.

ANDANTE & RONDO
from
GRAND SONATA IN D MINOR
Op. 49.
BY
C. M. von WEBER.

Ent. Sta. Hall.

Price 6s/=

FORSYTH BROTHERS,
272a Regent Circus, Oxford Street, London,
Cross Street and South King Street, Manchester.

PREFACE.

A few remarks will suffice to explain the object of this Publication and its distinguishing features.

"THE PRACTICAL PIANOFORTE SCHOOL." will consist of a series of Pieces selected from the best Composers, and calculated to guide students, by gradual steps, from the very beginning to the highest degree of execution, and at the same time to form their taste and style.

The Work will be divided into five sections, namely, ELEMENTARY, EASY, MODERATELY DIFFICULT, DIFFICULT, and *VERY DIFFICULT. Commencing with the rudiments of Musical Notation, the Pieces will succeed each other in such progressive order that Students, after having mastered one number, may safely proceed to the next, thus sparing both Teacher and Pupil the difficult task of selection.

Each Piece will be prefaced by a certain number of Exercises written expressly by me for this Publication, and having some bearing upon the difficulties of the Composition which they introduce. The daily practice of these Exercises should always precede that of the piece, until both are completely mastered.

Long experience has convinced me that the usual mode of fingering is insufficient to guard Pupils from the danger of contracting bad habits, as they cannot always be under the eye of the Master, and yet require a *constant* guide in this more than in any other matter. *Every note therefore will be fingered*, except that in the case of reiterated chords the fingering will be marked only once, and Octaves will not be fingered when they are to be played with the thumb and fourth finger.

All *Turns, Shakes, Appoggiaturas*, and other Ornaments, will be clearly explained in foot-notes, whenever their proper execution may be doubtful; and in the more advanced pieces there will be found, in brackets, *supplementary signs of expression*, where they may appear to me to facilitate the correct rendering of the Composer's intention. These I give on my own responsibility, and as my interpretation of the master-pieces which I have made my study for many years.

Two Metronome marks will be prefixed to every Piece and Exercise;—the first indicating the time beyond which Students ought not to venture before they can play both Piece and Exercise without fault; and the second giving the correct time.

The utmost endeavours will be used to keep the entire Work free from errors, and the greatest care bestowed upon its publication, which the long and intimate relations I have had with Messrs FORSYTH BROTHERS have led me to entrust to them.

A long experience as a Teacher and Performer, and a thorough acquaintance with the whole range of Pianoforte Music, encourage me in the hope that this "Practical Pianoforte School" may prove what I wish it to be—a safe guide towards a sound Musical Education.

CHARLES HALLE.

---

* The title "Very Difficult" is not meant to convey the idea that this Section will provide pieces of the extreme difficulty suited to exceptional cases only (this being beyond the scope of a "*School*"); it is by taxing in a high degree the general Students' *intellectual* faculties, as well as their mechanical powers, that the works included will be found "*very difficult*" to play well.

DAILY EXERCISES.
Each repeat to be played twenty times without stopping.

ANDANTE AND RONDO.

From Sonata in D minor.

C. M. von WEBER. Op. 49.

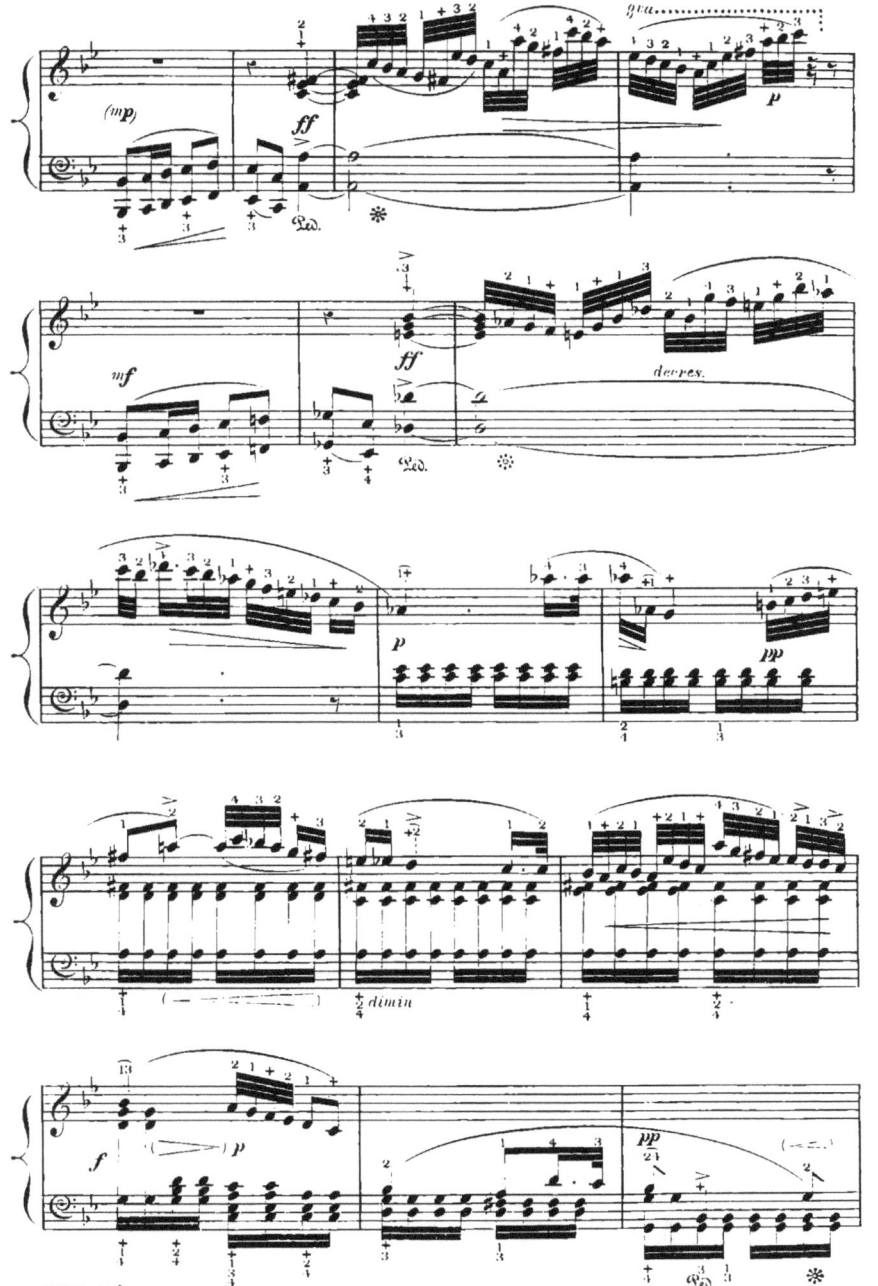

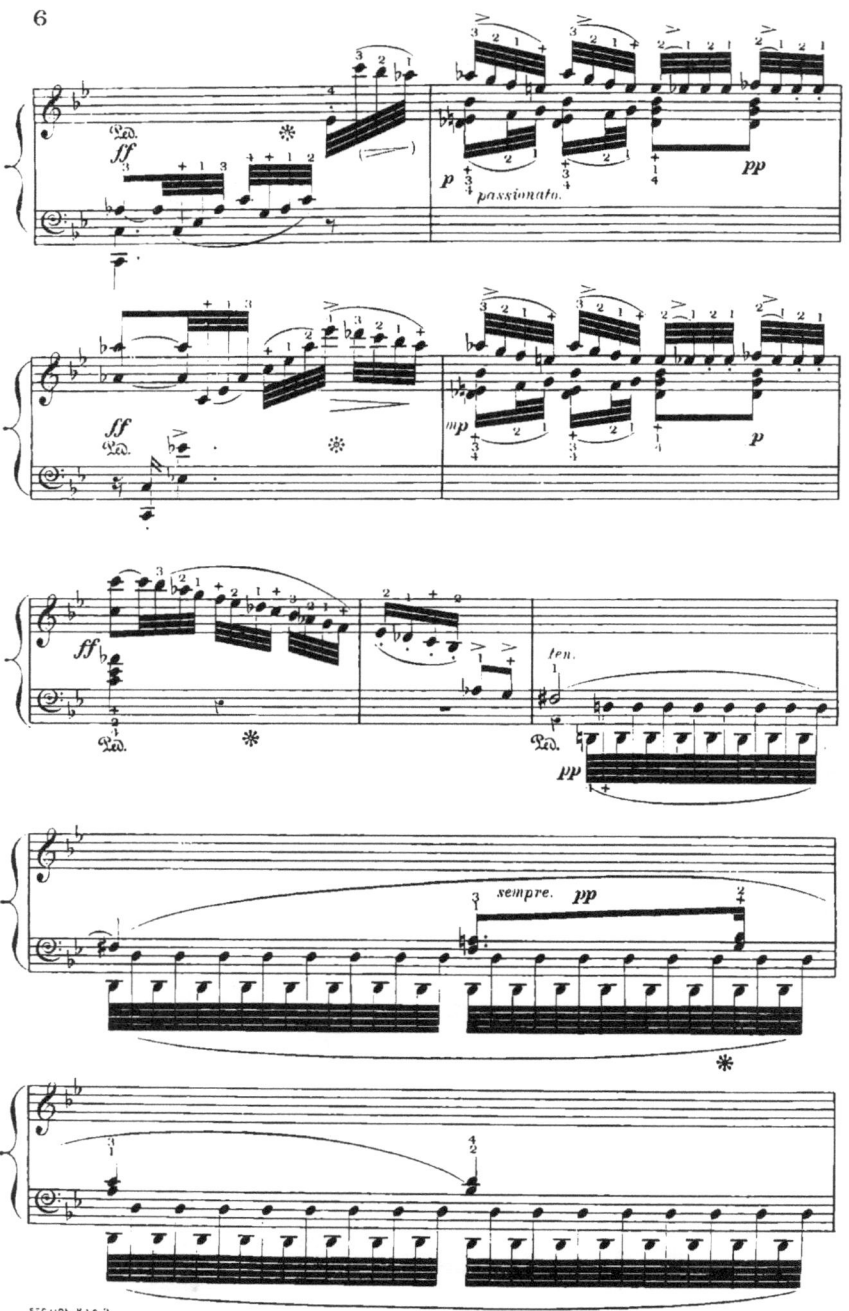

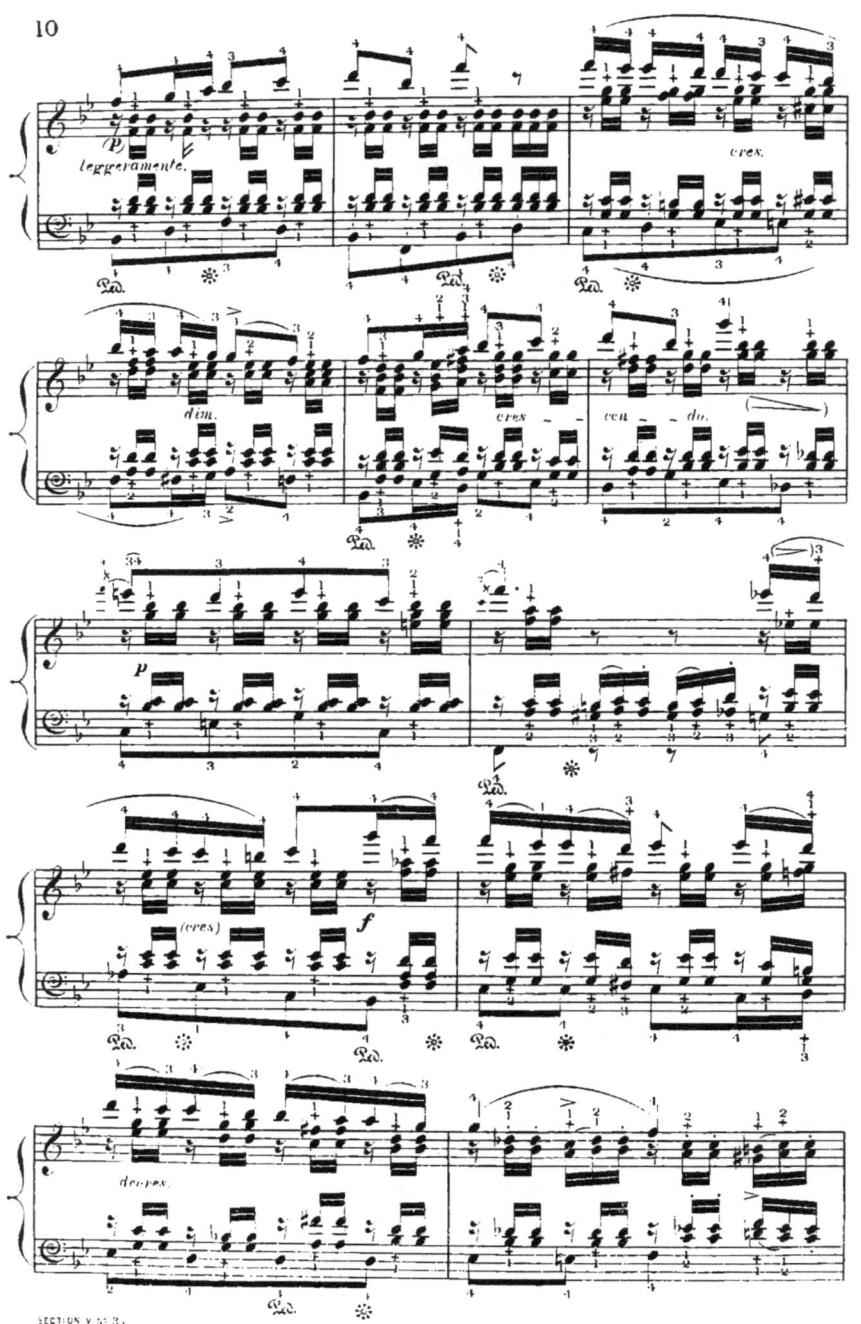

RONDO.

SECTION V N° 3.

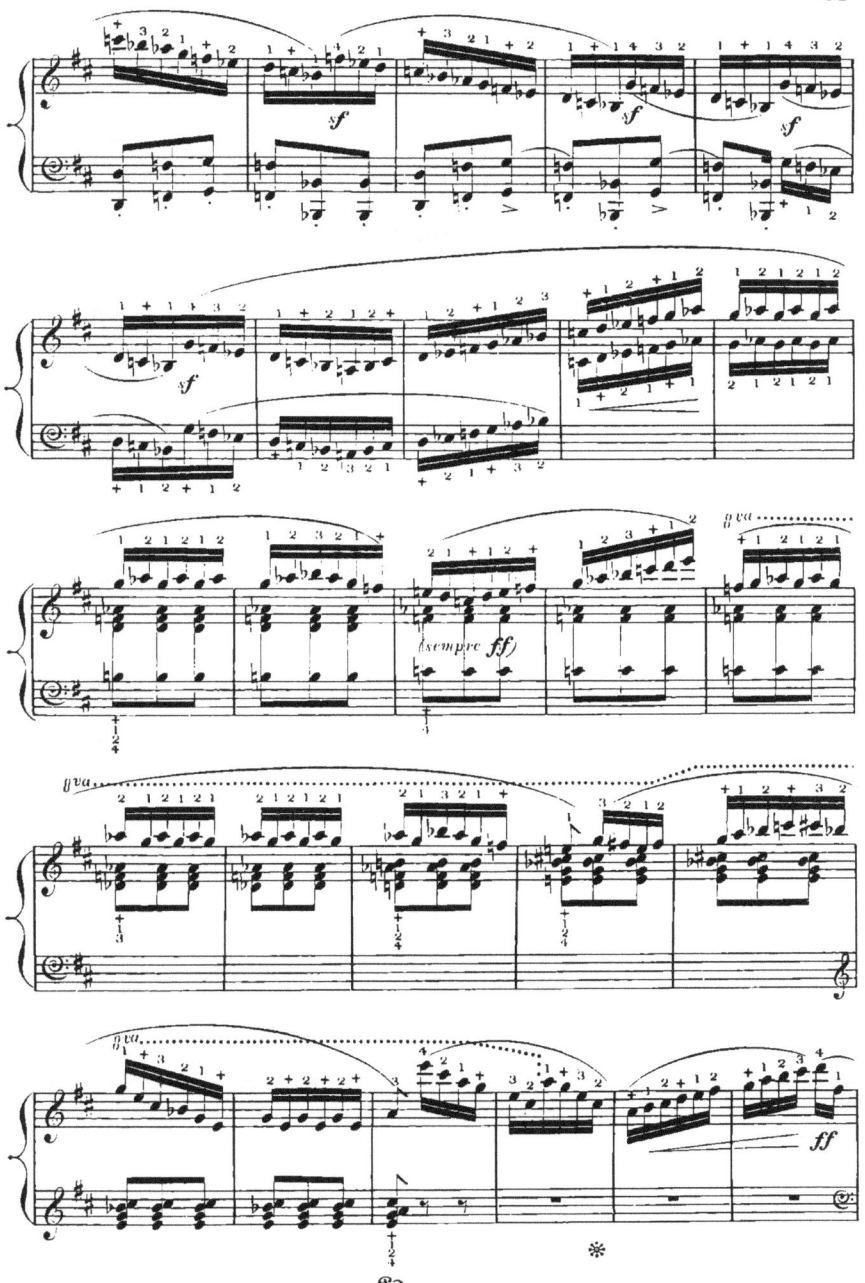

24

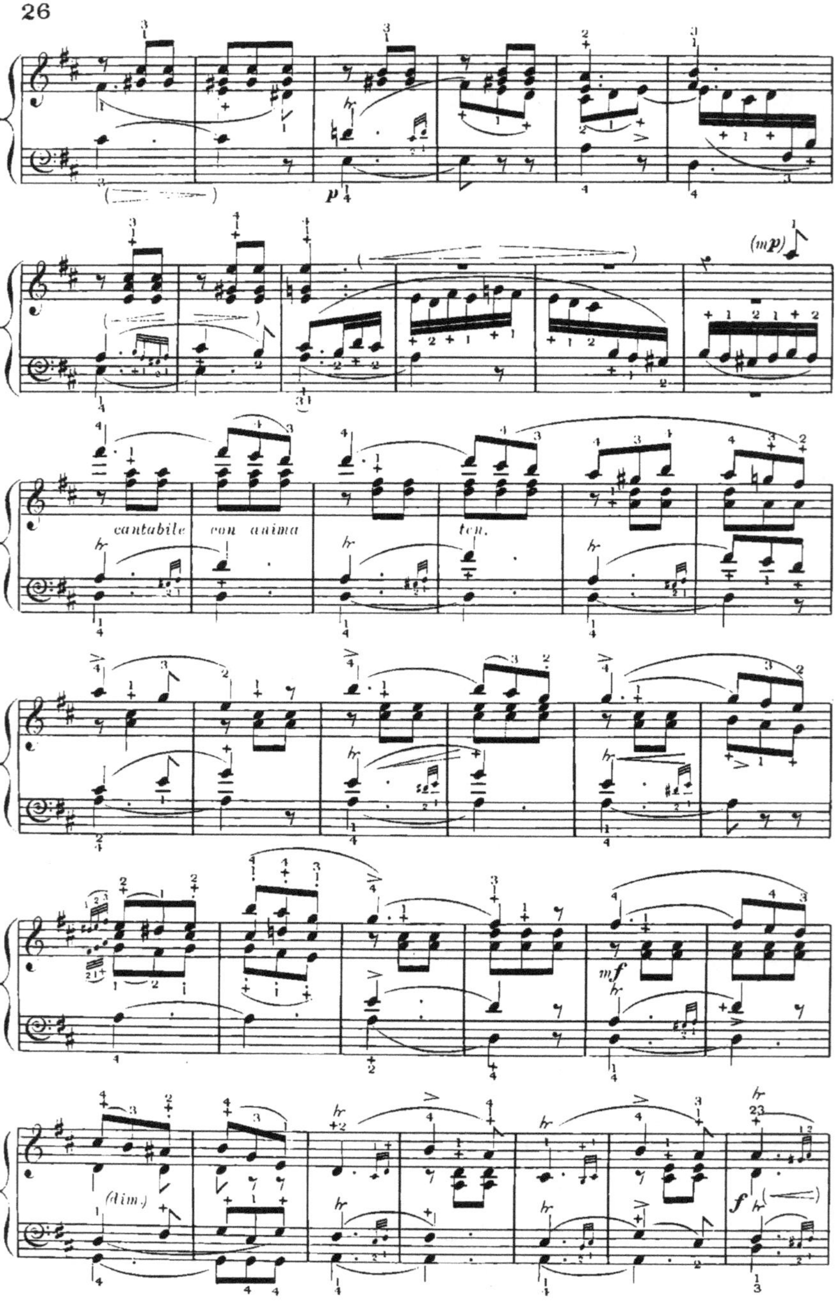
(mp)
cantabile
con anima
ten.
mf
(dim.)
f

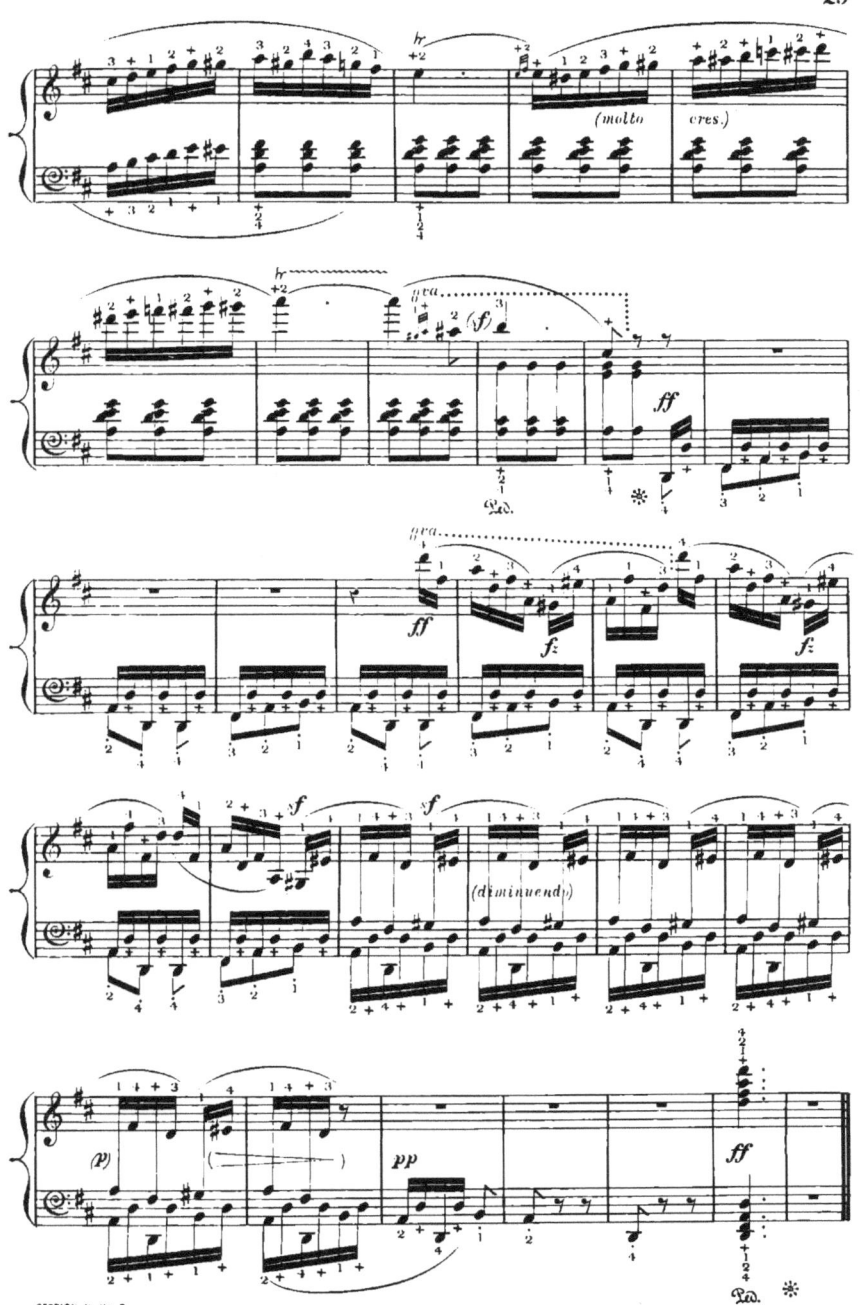

SECTION V. Nº 4.

CHARLES HALLÉ'S
PRACTICAL
Pianoforte School.

LA CHASSE
STUDY IN E FLAT,
Op. 29.
BY
STEPHEN HELLER.

ENT. STA. HALL.

PRICE 4/6

FORSYTH BROTHERS,
27.2ª Regent Circus Oxford Street, London
AND
Cross Street and South King Street, Manchester.

A few remarks will suffice to explain the object of this Publication and its distinguishing features.

"THE PRACTICAL PIANOFORTE SCHOOL," will consist of a series of Pieces selected from the best Composers, and calculated to guide students, by gradual steps, from the very beginning to the highest degree of execution, and at the same time to form their taste and style.

The Work will be divided into five sections, namely, ELEMENTARY, EASY, MODERATELY DIFFICULT, DIFFICULT, and *VERY DIFFICULT. Commencing with the rudiments of Musical Notation, the Pieces will succeed each other in such progressive order that Students, after having mastered one number, may safely proceed to the next, thus sparing both Teacher and Pupil the difficult task of selection.

Each Piece will be prefaced by a certain number of Exercises written expressly by me for this Publication, and having some bearing upon the difficulties of the Composition which they introduce. The daily practice of these Exercises should always precede that of the piece, until both are completely mastered.

Long experience has convinced me that the usual mode of fingering is insufficient to guard Pupils from the danger of contracting bad habits, as they cannot always be under the eye of the Master, and yet require a *constant* guide in this more than in any other matter. *Every note therefore will be fingered*, except that in the case of reiterated chords the fingering will be marked only once, and Octaves will not be fingered when they are to be played with the thumb and fourth finger.

All *Turns, Shakes, Appoggiaturas,* and other Ornaments, will be clearly explained in foot-notes, whenever their proper execution may be doubtful; and in the more advanced pieces there will be found, in brackets, *supplementary signs of expression,* where they may appear to me to facilitate the correct rendering of the Composer's intention. These I give on my own responsibility, and as my interpretation of the master-pieces which I have made my study for many years.

Two Metronome marks will be prefixed to every Piece and Exercise;—the first indicating the time beyond which Students ought not to venture before they can play both Piece and Exercise without fault; and the second giving the correct time.

The utmost endeavours will be used to keep the entire Work free from errors, and the greatest care bestowed upon its publication, which the long and intimate relations I have had with Messrs FORSYTH BROTHERS have led me to entrust to them.

A long experience as a Teacher and Performer, and a thorough acquaintance with the whole range of Pianoforte Music, encourage me in the hope that this "Practical Pianoforte School" may prove what I wish it to be — a safe guide towards a sound Musical Education.

CHARLES HALLE.

* The title "Very Difficult" is not meant to convey the idea that this Section will provide pieces of the extreme difficulty suited to exceptional cases only (this being beyond the scope of a "*School*"); it is by taxing in a high degree the general Students' intellectual faculties, as well as their mechanical powers, that the works included will be found "*very difficult*" to play well.

DAILY EXERCISES.
Each repeat to be played six times without stopping.

LA CHASSE.

ETUDE.

("La meute est déchaînée, les fanfares éclatent. Messire le Roi Philippe, sur son ardent coursier, s'efforce à dissiper le chagrin que lui cause le trépas de sa mie Agnès de Méranie.") (BALLADE DE HUET LE NORMAND.)

S. HELLER Op. 29.

SECTION V. N° 5.

CHARLES HALLÉ'S
PRACTICAL
Pianoforte School.

SONATA
"LES ADIEUX, L'ABSENCE ET LE RETOUR"
Op. 81.
BY
L. VAN BEETHOVEN.

ENT STA HALL

PRICE 6⁄s

FORSYTH BROTHERS,
2729 Regent Circus, Oxford Street, London
Cross Street and South King Street, Manchester

A few remarks will suffice to explain the object of this Publication and its distinguishing features.

"THE PRACTICAL PIANOFORTE SCHOOL" will consist of a series of Pieces selected from the best Composers, and calculated to guide students, by gradual steps, from the very beginning to the highest degree of execution, and at the same time to form their taste and style.

The Work will be divided into five sections, namely, ELEMENTARY, EASY, MODERATELY DIFFICULT, DIFFICULT, and *VERY DIFFICULT. Commencing with the rudiments of Musical Notation, the Pieces will succeed each other in such progressive order that Students, after having mastered one number, may safely proceed to the next, thus sparing both Teacher and Pupil the difficult task of selection.

Each Piece will be prefaced by a certain number of Exercises written expressly by me for this Publication, and having some bearing upon the difficulties of the Composition which they introduce. The daily practice of these Exercises should always precede that of the piece, until both are completely mastered.

Long experience has convinced me that the usual mode of fingering is insufficient to guard Pupils from the danger of contracting bad habits, as they cannot always be under the eye of the Master, and yet require a *constant* guide in this more than in any other matter. *Every note therefore will be fingered,* except that in the case of reiterated chords the fingering will be marked only once, and Octaves will not be fingered when they are to be played with the thumb and fourth finger.

All *Turns, Shakes, Appoggiaturas,* and other Ornaments, will be clearly explained in foot-notes, whenever their proper execution may be doubtful; and in the more advanced pieces there will be found, in brackets, *supplementary signs of expression,* where they may appear to me to facilitate the correct rendering of the Composer's intention. These I give on my own responsibility, and as my interpretation of the master-pieces which I have made my study for many years.

Two Metronome marks will be prefixed to every Piece and Exercise;—the first indicating the time beyond which Students ought not to venture before they can play both Piece and Exercise without fault; and the second giving the correct time.

The utmost endeavours will be used to keep the entire Work free from errors, and the greatest care bestowed upon its publication, which the long and intimate relations I have had with Messrs FORSYTH BROTHERS have led me to entrust to them.

A long experience as a Teacher and Performer, and a thorough acquaintance with the whole range of Pianoforte Music, encourage me in the hope that this "Practical Pianoforte School" may prove what I wish it to be—a safe guide towards a sound Musical Education.

CHARLES HALLÉ.

* The title "Very Difficult" is not meant to convey the idea that this Section will provide pieces of the extreme difficulty suited to exceptional cases only (this being beyond the scope of a "*School*"); it is by taxing in a high degree the general Students' *intellectual* faculties, as well as their mechanical powers, that the works included will be found "*very difficult*" to play well.

DAILY EXERCISES.

Each repeat to be played twelve times without stopping.

SONATA.

LES ADIEUX.

L. van BEETHOVEN. Op. 81.

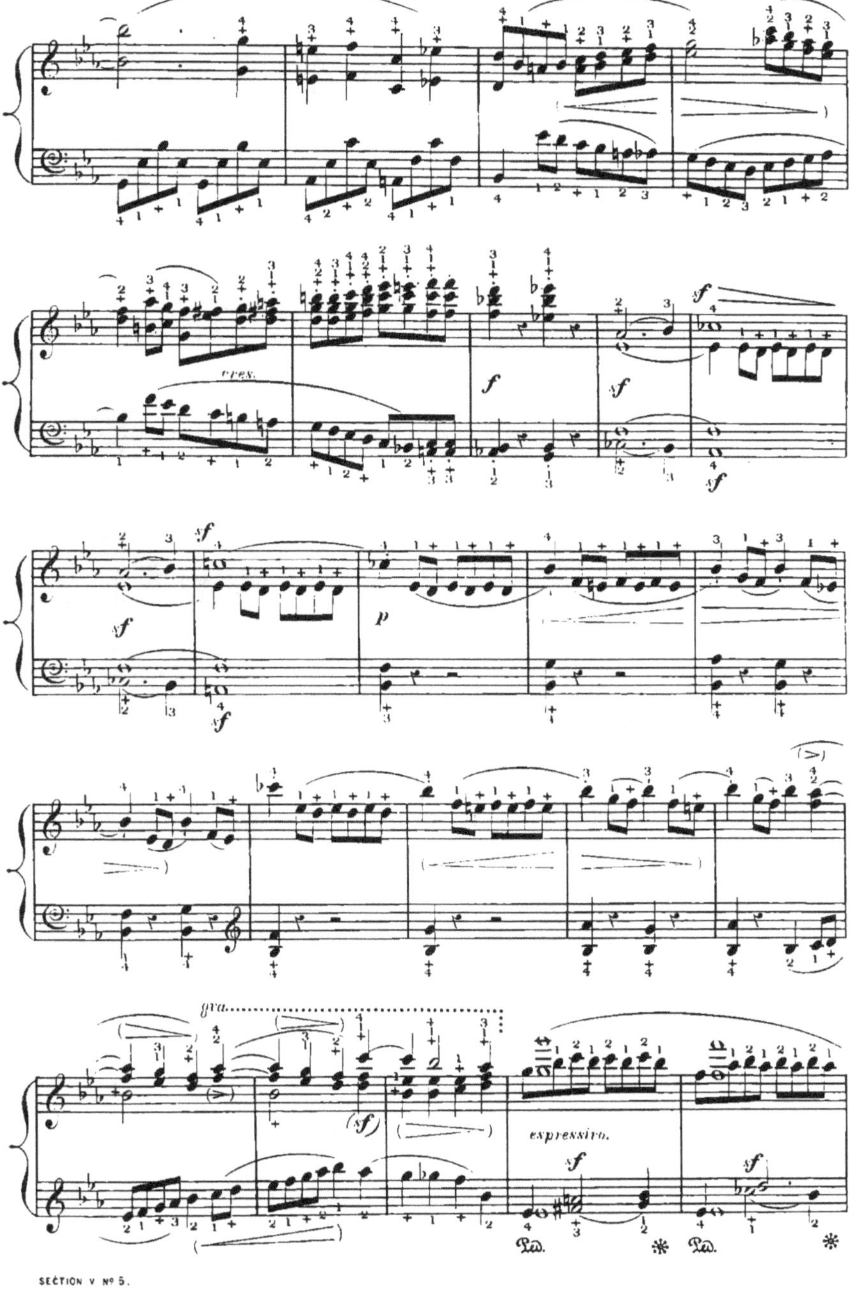
cres.
f
sf
p
8va
espressivo.
Ped.

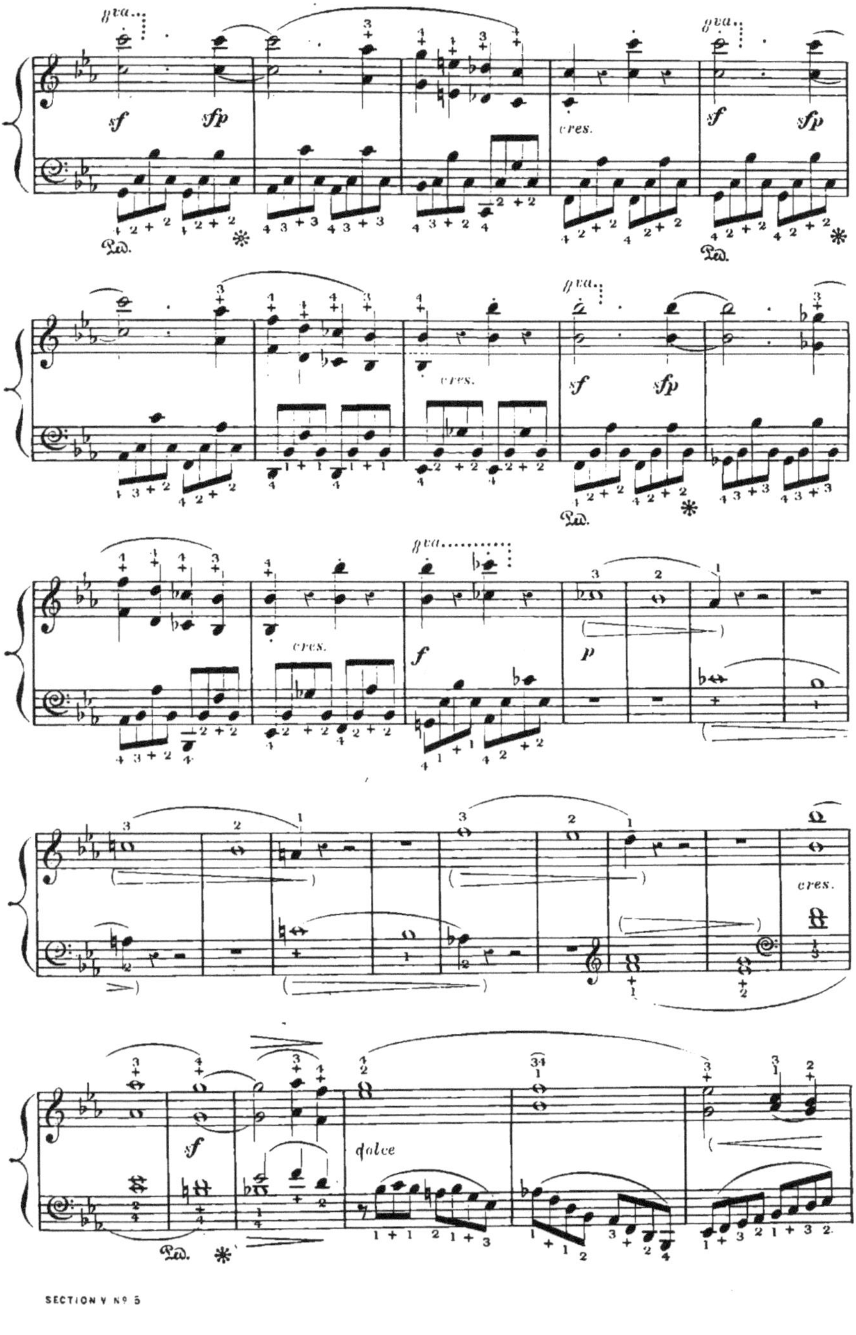
8va
sf
sfp
cres.
Ped.
p
f
dolce

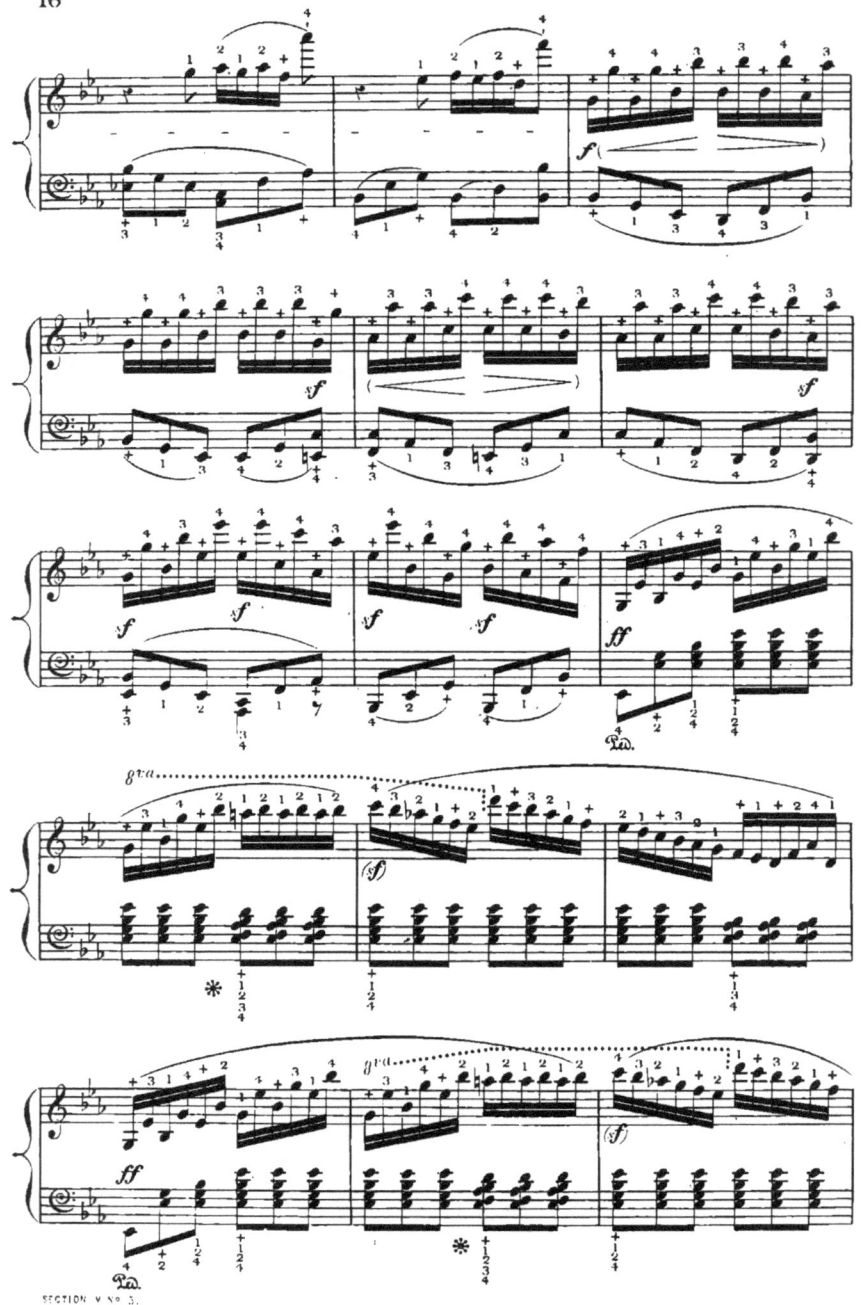

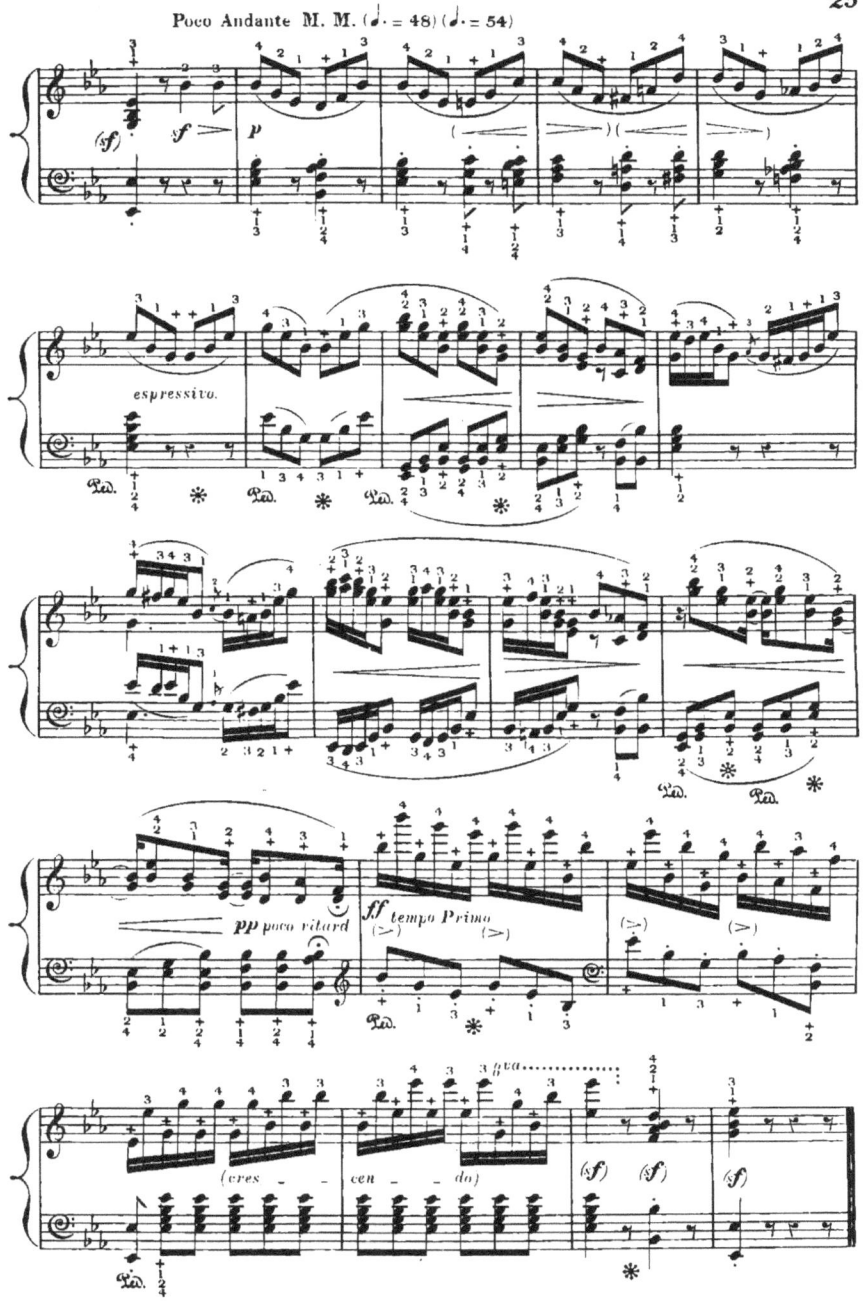

SECTION V. N°6.

CHARLES HALLÉ'S
PRACTICAL
Pianoforte School.

PRESTO SCHERZANDO
IN
F SHARP MINOR,
BY
F. MENDELSSOHN.

ENT STA HALL

PRICE 4/=

FORSYTH BROTHERS.
272.ᵃ Regent Circus, Oxford Street, London
AND
Cross Street and South King Street, Manchester

A few remarks will suffice to explain the object of this Publication and its distinguishing features.

"THE PRACTICAL PIANOFORTE SCHOOL" will consist of a series of Pieces selected from the best Composers, and calculated to guide students, by gradual steps, from the very beginning to the highest degree of execution, and at the same time to form their taste and style.

The Work will be divided into five sections, namely, ELEMENTARY, EASY, MODERATELY DIFFICULT, DIFFICULT, and *VERY DIFFICULT. Commencing with the rudiments of Musical Notation, the Pieces will succeed each other in such progressive order that Students, after having mastered one number, may safely proceed to the next, thus sparing both Teacher and Pupil the difficult task of selection.

Each Piece will be prefaced by a certain number of Exercises written expressly by me for this Publication, and having some bearing upon the difficulties of the Composition which they introduce. The daily practice of these Exercises should always precede that of the piece, until both are completely mastered.

Long experience has convinced me that the usual mode of fingering is insufficient to guard Pupils from the danger of contracting bad habits, as they cannot always be under the eye of the Master, and yet require a *constant* guide in this more than in any other matter. *Every note therefore will be fingered*, except that in the case of reiterated chords the fingering will be marked only once, and Octaves will not be fingered when they are to be played with the thumb and fourth finger.

All *Turns, Shakes, Appoggiaturas*, and other Ornaments, will be clearly explained in foot-notes, whenever their proper execution may be doubtful; and in the more advanced pieces there will be found, in brackets, *supplementary signs of expression*, where they may appear to me to facilitate the correct rendering of the Composer's intention. These I give on my own responsibility, and as my interpretation of the master-pieces which I have made my study for many years.

Two Metronome marks will be prefixed to every Piece and Exercise;—the first indicating the time beyond which Students ought not to venture before they can play both Piece and Exercise without fault; and the second giving the correct time.

The utmost endeavours will be used to keep the entire Work free from errors, and the greatest care bestowed upon its publication, which the long and intimate relations I have had with Messrs FORSYTH BROTHERS have led me to entrust to them.

A long experience as a Teacher and Performer, and a thorough acquaintance with the whole range of Pianoforte Music, encourage me in the hope that this "Practical Pianoforte School" may prove what I wish it to be—a safe guide towards a sound Musical Education.

CHARLES HALLÉ.

* The title "Very Difficult" is not meant to convey the idea that this Section will provide pieces of the extreme difficulty suited to exceptional cases only (this being beyond the scope of a "*School*"); it is by taxing in a high degree the general Students' *intellectual* faculties, as well as their mechanical powers, that the works included will be found "*very difficult*" to play well.

DAILY EXERCISES.
Each repeat to be played six times without stopping.

PRESTO SCHERZANDO.

M.M. (♩. = 104.) (♩. = 126.) MENDELSSOHN BARTHOLDY.

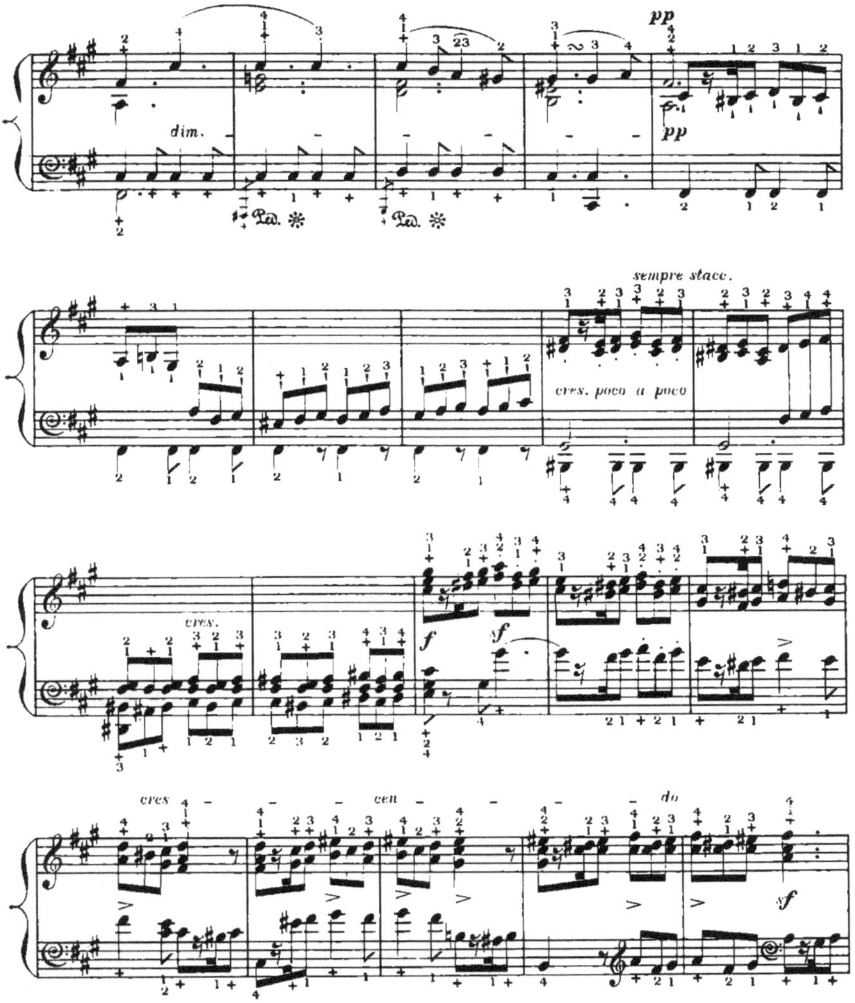
pp
dim.
pp
Ped.
Ped.
sempre stacc.
cres. poco a poco
cres.
f
sf
cres - - cen - - - do
sf
f
sf
sf
f
sf
sf
sf

SECTION V. Nº 7.

CHARLES HALLÉ'S
PRACTICAL
Pianoforte School.

TWO STUDIES
IN E & G FLAT,
from Op. 10.
BY
F. CHOPIN.

ENT. STA. HALL.   PRICE 4/=

FORSYTH BROTHERS.
272.ª Regent Circus, Oxford Street, London
Cross Street and South King Street, Manchester.

A few remarks will suffice to explain the object of this Publication and its distinguishing features.

"THE PRACTICAL PIANOFORTE SCHOOL," will consist of a series of Pieces selected from the best Composers, and calculated to guide students, by gradual steps, from the very beginning to the highest degree of execution, and at the same time to form their taste and style.

The Work will be divided into five sections, namely, ELEMENTARY, EASY, MODERATELY DIFFICULT, DIFFICULT, and *VERY DIFFICULT. Commencing with the rudiments of Musical Notation, the Pieces will succeed each other in such progressive order that Students, after having mastered one number, may safely proceed to the next, thus sparing both Teacher and Pupil the difficult task of selection.

Each Piece will be prefaced by a certain number of Exercises written expressly by me for this Publication, and having some bearing upon the difficulties of the Composition which they introduce. The daily practice of these Exercises should always precede that of the piece, until both are completely mastered.

Long experience has convinced me that the usual mode of fingering is insufficient to guard Pupils from the danger of contracting bad habits, as they cannot always be under the eye of the Master, and yet require a *constant* guide in this more than in any other matter. *Every note therefore will be fingered*, except that in the case of reiterated chords the fingering will be marked only once, and Octaves will not be fingered when they are to be played with the thumb and fourth finger.

All *Turns, Shakes, Appoggiaturas*, and other Ornaments, will be clearly explained in foot-notes, whenever their proper execution may be doubtful; and in the more advanced pieces there will be found, in brackets, *supplementary signs of expression*, where they may appear to me to facilitate the correct rendering of the Composer's intention. These I give on my own responsibility, and as my interpretation of the master-pieces which I have made my study for many years.

Two Metronome marks will be prefixed to every Piece and Exercise;—the first indicating the time beyond which Students ought not to venture before they can play both Piece and Exercise without fault; and the second giving the correct time.

The utmost endeavours will be used to keep the entire Work free from errors, and the greatest care bestowed upon its publication, which the long and intimate relations I have had with Messrs FORSYTH BROTHERS have led me to entrust to them.

A long experience as a Teacher and Performer, and a thorough acquaintance with the whole range of Pianoforte Music, encourage me in the hope that this "Practical Pianoforte School" may prove what I wish it to be—a safe guide towards a sound Musical Education.

CHARLES HALLE.

* The title "Very Difficult" is not meant to convey the idea that this Section will provide pieces of the extreme difficulty suited to exceptional cases only (this being beyond the scope of a "*School*"); it is by taxing in a high degree the general Students' *intellectual* faculties, as well as their mechanical powers, that the works included will be found "*very difficult*" to play well.

DAILY EXERCISES.
Each repeat to be played ten times without stopping.

8

SECTION V Nº 7.

SECTION V. N? 8.

CHARLES HALLÉ'S
PRACTICAL
Pianoforte School.

MOMENTO CAPRICCIOSO
IN B FLAT,
Op. 12,
BY
C. M. VON WEBER.

ENT. STA. HALL.   PRICE 4/0

FORSYTH BROTHERS,
272° Regent Circus, Oxford Street, London
Cross Street and South King Street, Manchester.

A few remarks will suffice to explain the object of this Publication and its distinguishing features.

"The Practical Pianoforte School," will consist of a series of Pieces selected from the best Composers, and calculated to guide students, by gradual steps, from the very beginning to the highest degree of execution, and at the same time to form their taste and style.

The Work will be divided into five sections, namely, Elementary, Easy, Moderately Difficult, Difficult, and *Very Difficult. Commencing with the rudiments of Musical Notation, the Pieces will succeed each other in such progressive order that Students, after having mastered one number, may safely proceed to the next, thus sparing both Teacher and Pupil the difficult task of selection.

Each Piece will be prefaced by a certain number of Exercises written expressly by me for this Publication, and having some bearing upon the difficulties of the Composition which they introduce. The daily practice of these Exercises should always precede that of the piece, until both are completely mastered.

Long experience has convinced me that the usual mode of fingering is insufficient to guard Pupils from the danger of contracting bad habits, as they cannot always be under the eye of the Master, and yet require a *constant* guide in this more than in any other matter. *Every note therefore will be fingered*, except that in the case of reiterated chords the fingering will be marked only once, and Octaves will not be fingered when they are to be played with the thumb and fourth finger.

All *Turns, Shakes, Appoggiaturas*, and other Ornaments, will be clearly explained in foot-notes, whenever their proper execution may be doubtful; and in the more advanced pieces there will be found, in brackets, *supplementary signs of expression*, where they may appear to me to facilitate the correct rendering of the Composer's intention. These I give on my own responsibility, and as my interpretation of the master-pieces which I have made my study for many years.

Two Metronome marks will be prefixed to every Piece and Exercise;—the first indicating the time beyond which Students ought not to venture before they can play both Piece and Exercise without fault; and the second giving the correct time.

The utmost endeavours will be used to keep the entire Work free from errors, and the greatest care bestowed upon its publication, which the long and intimate relations I have had with Messrs Forsyth Brothers have led me to entrust to them.

A long experience as a Teacher and Performer, and a thorough acquaintance with the whole range of Pianoforte Music, encourage me in the hope that this "Practical Pianoforte School" may prove what I wish it to be—a safe guide towards a sound Musical Education.

CHARLES HALLÉ.

---

* The title "Very Difficult" is not meant to convey the idea that this Section will provide pieces of the extreme difficulty suited to exceptional cases only (this being beyond the scope of a "*School*"); it is by taxing in a high degree the general Students' *intellectual* faculties, as well as their mechanical powers, that the works included will be found "*very difficult*" to play well.

DAILY EXERCISES.
Each repeat to be played six times without stopping.

MOMENTO CAPRICCIOSO.

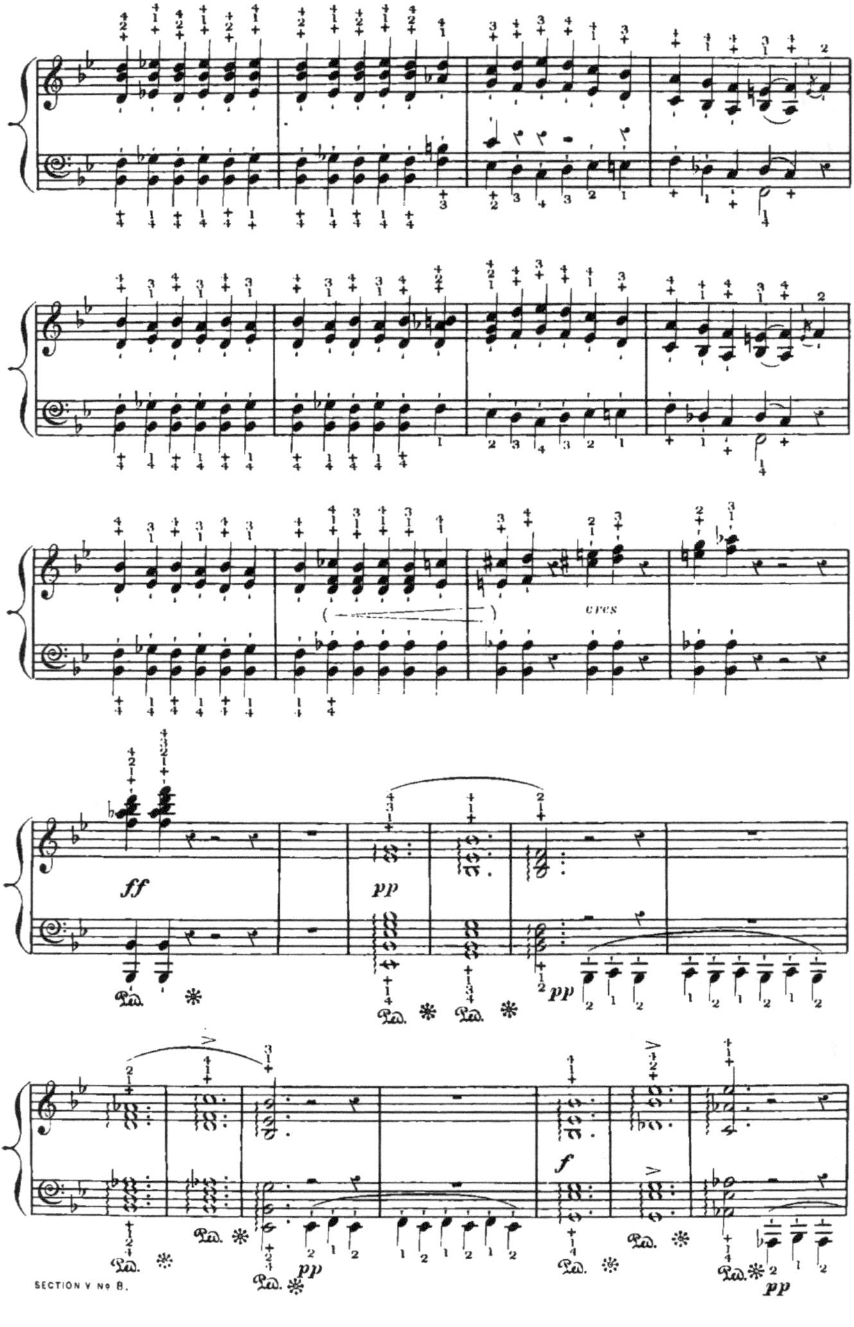

1

SECTION V. Nº 9

CHARLES HALLÉ'S
PRACTICAL
Pianoforte School.

FANTASIA CHROMATICA
IN D MINOR,
BY
J. S. BACH.

ENT. STA. HALL.   PRICE 5s/-

FORSYTH BROTHERS,
272ª Regent Circus, Oxford Street, London.
Cross Street and South King Street, Manchester.

A few remarks will suffice to explain the object of this Publication and its distinguishing features.

"THE PRACTICAL PIANOFORTE SCHOOL." will consist of a series of Pieces selected from the best Composers, and calculated to guide students, by gradual steps, from the very beginning to the highest degree of execution, and at the same time to form their taste and style.

The Work will be divided into five sections, namely, ELEMENTARY, EASY, MODERATELY DIFFICULT, DIFFICULT, and *VERY DIFFICULT. Commencing with the rudiments of Musical Notation, the Pieces will succeed each other in such progressive order that Students, after having mastered one number, may safely proceed to the next, thus sparing both Teacher and Pupil the difficult task of selection.

Each Piece will be prefaced by a certain number of Exercises written expressly by me for this Publication, and having some bearing upon the difficulties of the Composition which they introduce. The daily practice of these Exercises should always precede that of the piece, until both are completely mastered.

Long experience has convinced me that the usual mode of fingering is insufficient to guard Pupils from the danger of contracting bad habits, as they cannot always be under the eye of the Master, and yet require a *constant* guide in this more than in any other matter. *Every note therefore will be fingered*, except that in the case of reiterated chords the fingering will be marked only once, and Octaves will not be fingered when they are to be played with the thumb and fourth finger.

All *Turns, Shakes, Appoggiaturas*, and other Ornaments, will be clearly explained in foot-notes, whenever their proper execution may be doubtful; and in the more advanced pieces there will be found, in brackets, *supplementary signs of expression*, where they may appear to me to facilitate the correct rendering of the Composer's intention. These I give on my own responsibility, and as my interpretation of the master-pieces which I have made my study for many years.

Two Metronome marks will be prefixed to every Piece and Exercise;—the first indicating the time beyond which Students ought not to venture before they can play both Piece and Exercise without fault; and the second giving the correct time.

The utmost endeavours will be used to keep the entire Work free from errors, and the greatest care bestowed upon its publication, which the long and intimate relations I have had with Messrs FORSYTH BROTHERS have led me to entrust to them.

A long experience as a Teacher and Performer, and a thorough acquaintance with the whole range of Pianoforte Music, encourage me in the hope that this "Practical Pianoforte School" may prove what I wish it to be—a safe guide towards a sound Musical Education.

CHARLES HALLÉ.

* The title "Very Difficult" is not meant to convey the idea that this Section will provide pieces of the extreme difficulty suited to exceptional cases only (this being beyond the scope of a "*School*"); it is by taxing in a high degree the general Students' *intellectual* faculties, as well as their mechanical powers, that the works included will be found "*very difficult*" to play well.

DAILY EXERCISES.
Each repeat to be played fifteen times without stopping.

FANTASIA CHROMATICA.

J. S. BACH.

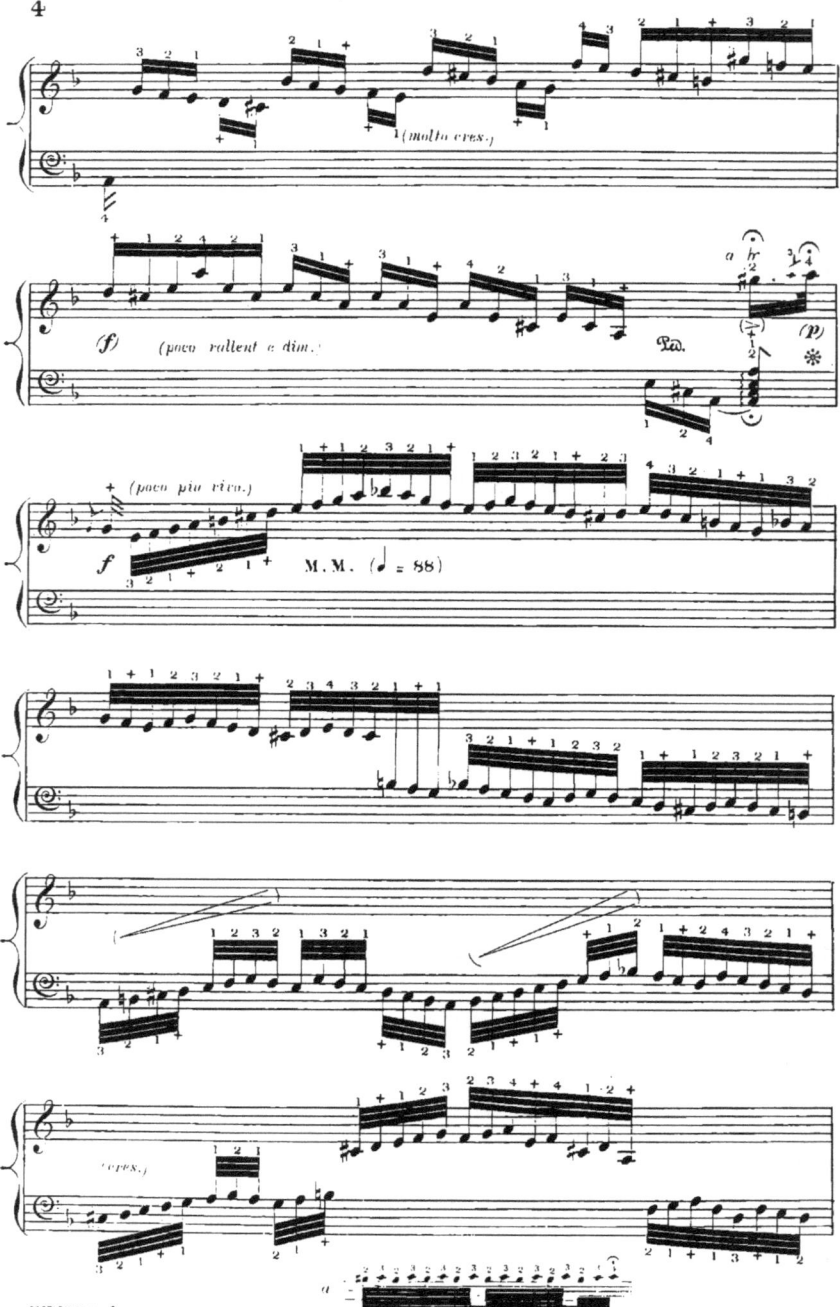

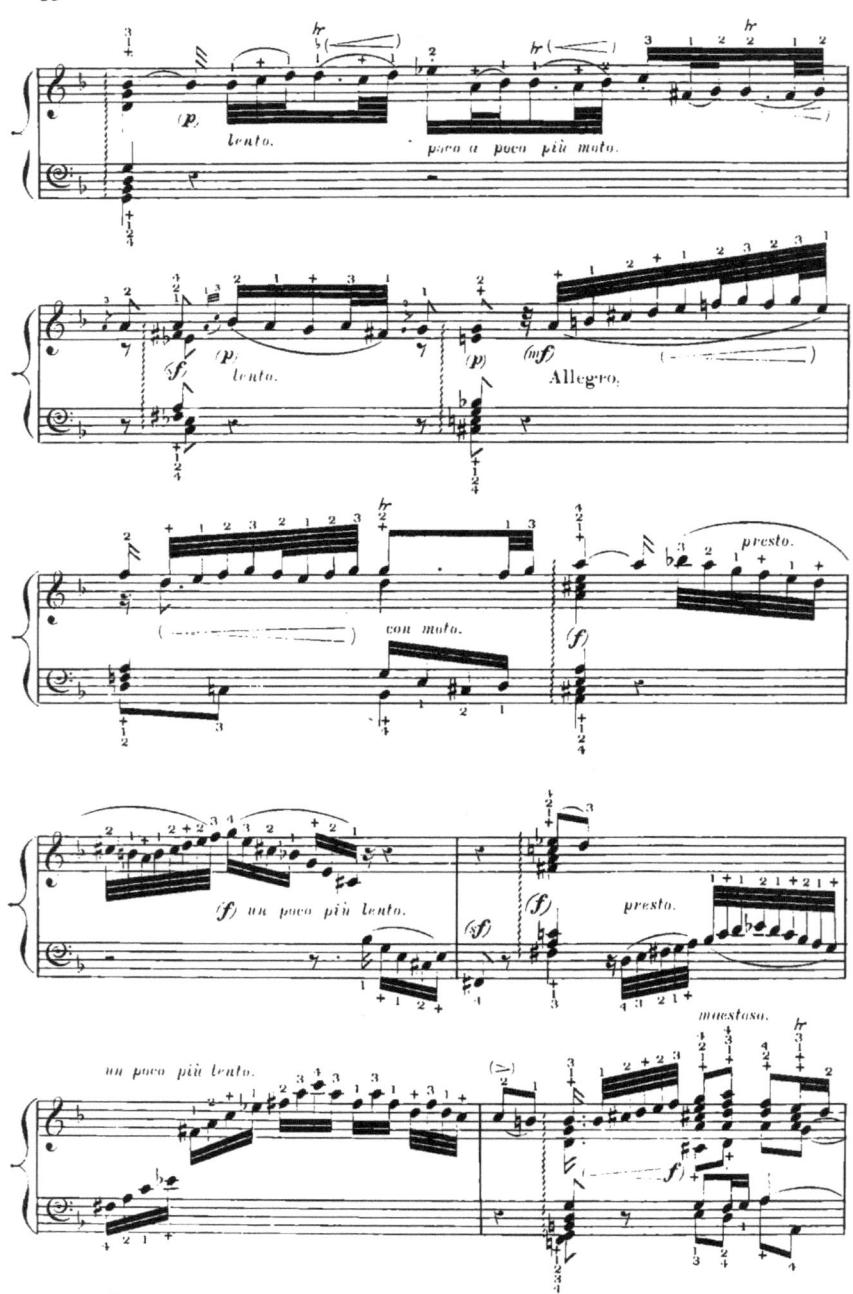

FUGA.
A tre Voci.

13

SECTION V No 9.

16

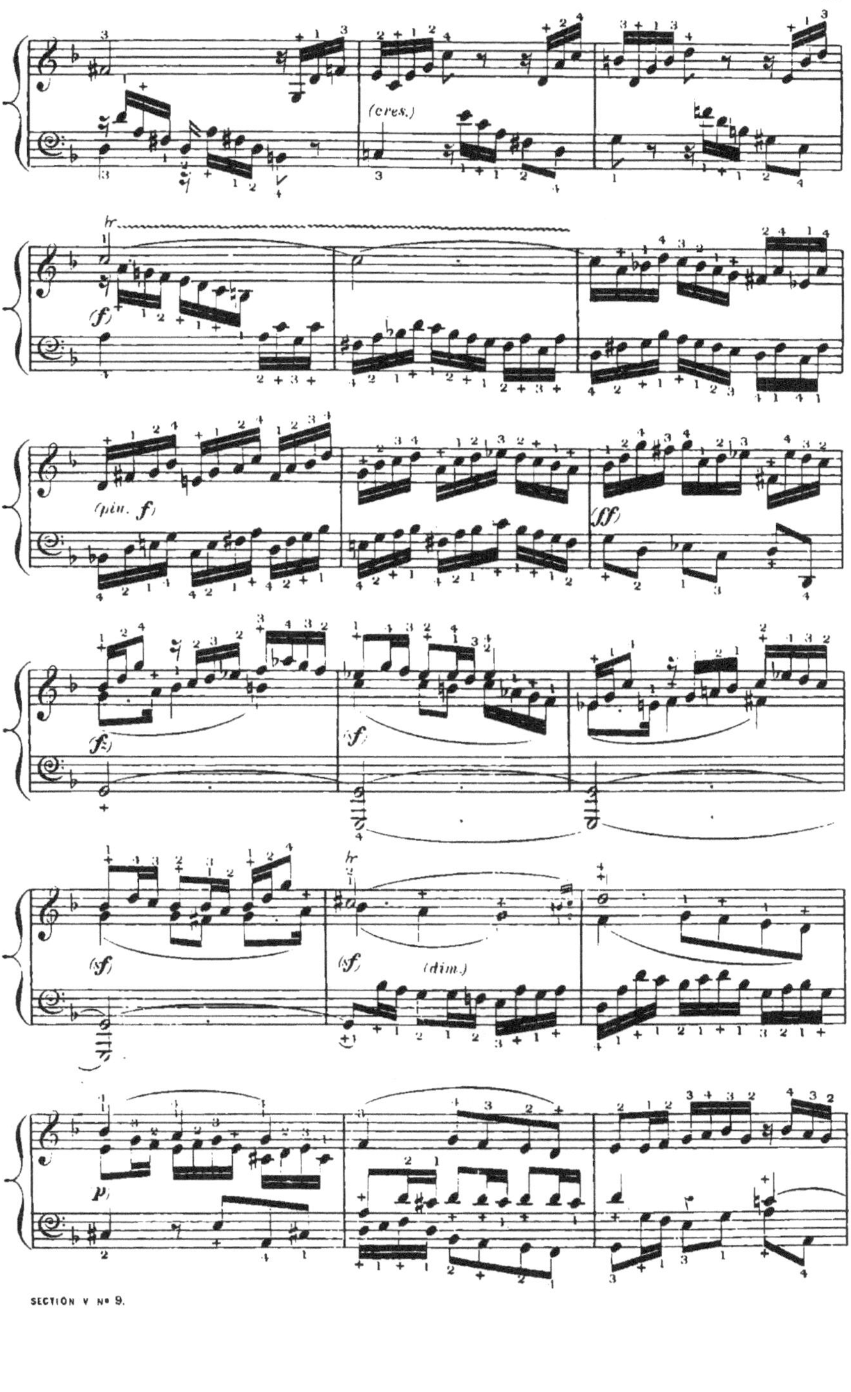
(cres.)
(f)
(più f)
(ff)
(fz)
(f)
(sf)
(sf)
(dim.)
p

SECTION V. N? 10

CHARLES HALLÉ'S
PRACTICAL
Pianoforte School.

ROMANZA
&
STUDY IN F SHARP,

from Op. 2.

BY

A. HENSELT.

Ent. Sta. Hall.   Price 4/0

FORSYTH BROTHERS,
27．9 Regent Circus, Oxford Street, London
AND
Cross Street and South King Street, Manchester.

A few remarks will suffice to explain the object of this Publication and its distinguishing features.

"THE PRACTICAL PIANOFORTE SCHOOL," will consist of a series of Pieces selected from the best Composers, and calculated to guide students, by gradual steps, from the very beginning to the highest degree of execution, and at the same time to form their taste and style.

The Work will be divided into five sections, namely, ELEMENTARY, EASY, MODERATELY DIFFICULT, DIFFICULT, and *VERY DIFFICULT. Commencing with the rudiments of Musical Notation, the Pieces will succeed each other in such progressive order that Students, after having mastered one number, may safely proceed to the next, thus sparing both Teacher and Pupil the difficult task of selection.

Each Piece will be prefaced by a certain number of Exercises written expressly by me for this Publication, and having some bearing upon the difficulties of the Composition which they introduce. The daily practice of these Exercises should always precede that of the piece, until both are completely mastered.

Long experience has convinced me that the usual mode of fingering is insufficient to guard Pupils from the danger of contracting bad habits, as they cannot always be under the eye of the Master, and yet require a *constant* guide in this more than in any other matter. *Every note therefore will be fingered*, except that in the case of reiterated chords the fingering will be marked only once, and Octaves will not be fingered when they are to be played with the thumb and fourth finger.

All *Turns*, *Shakes*, *Appoggiaturas*, and other Ornaments, will be clearly explained in foot-notes, whenever their proper execution may be doubtful; and in the more advanced pieces there will be found, in brackets, *supplementary signs of expression*, where they may appear to me to facilitate the correct rendering of the Composer's intention. These I give on my own responsibility, and as my interpretation of the master-pieces which I have made my study for many years.

Two *Metronome marks* will be prefixed to every Piece and Exercise;—the first indicating the time beyond which Students ought not to venture before they can play both Piece and Exercise without fault; and the second giving the correct time.

The utmost endeavours will be used to keep the entire Work free from errors, and the greatest care bestowed upon its publication, which the long and intimate relations I have had with Messrs FORSYTH BROTHERS have led me to entrust to them.

A long experience as a Teacher and Performer, and a thorough acquaintance with the whole range of Pianoforte Music, encourage me in the hope that this "Practical Pianoforte School" may prove what I wish it to be—a safe guide towards a sound Musical Education.

CHARLES HALLÉ.

* The title "Very Difficult" is not meant to convey the idea that this Section will provide pieces of the extreme difficulty suited to exceptional cases only (this being beyond the scope of a "*School*"); it is by taxing in a high degree the general Students' *intellectual* faculties, as well as their mechanical powers, that the works included will be found "*very difficult*" to play well.

DAILY EXERCISES.

Each repeat to be played ten times without stopping.

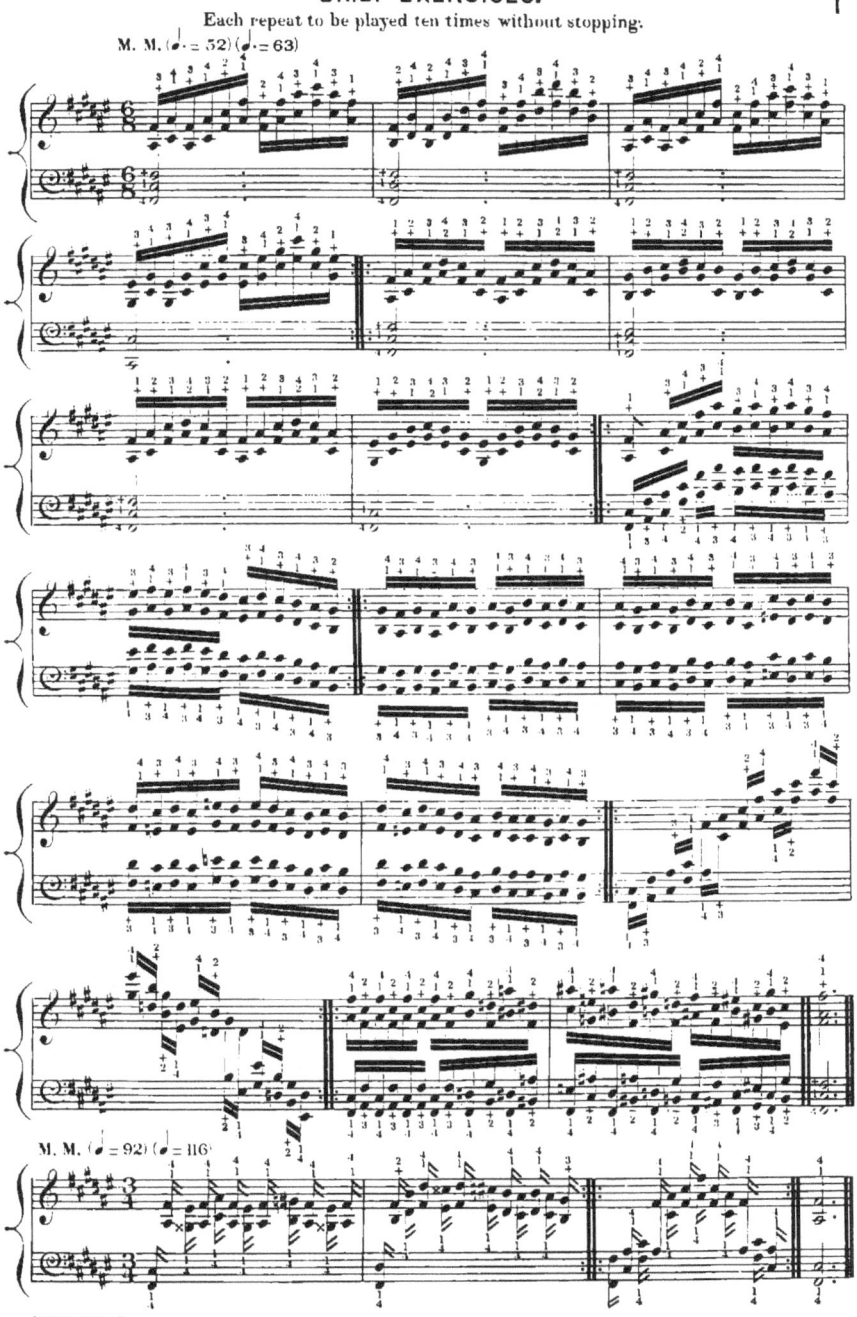

ROMANZA
In B flat minor
&
STUDY
In F sharp major.

A. HENSELT.

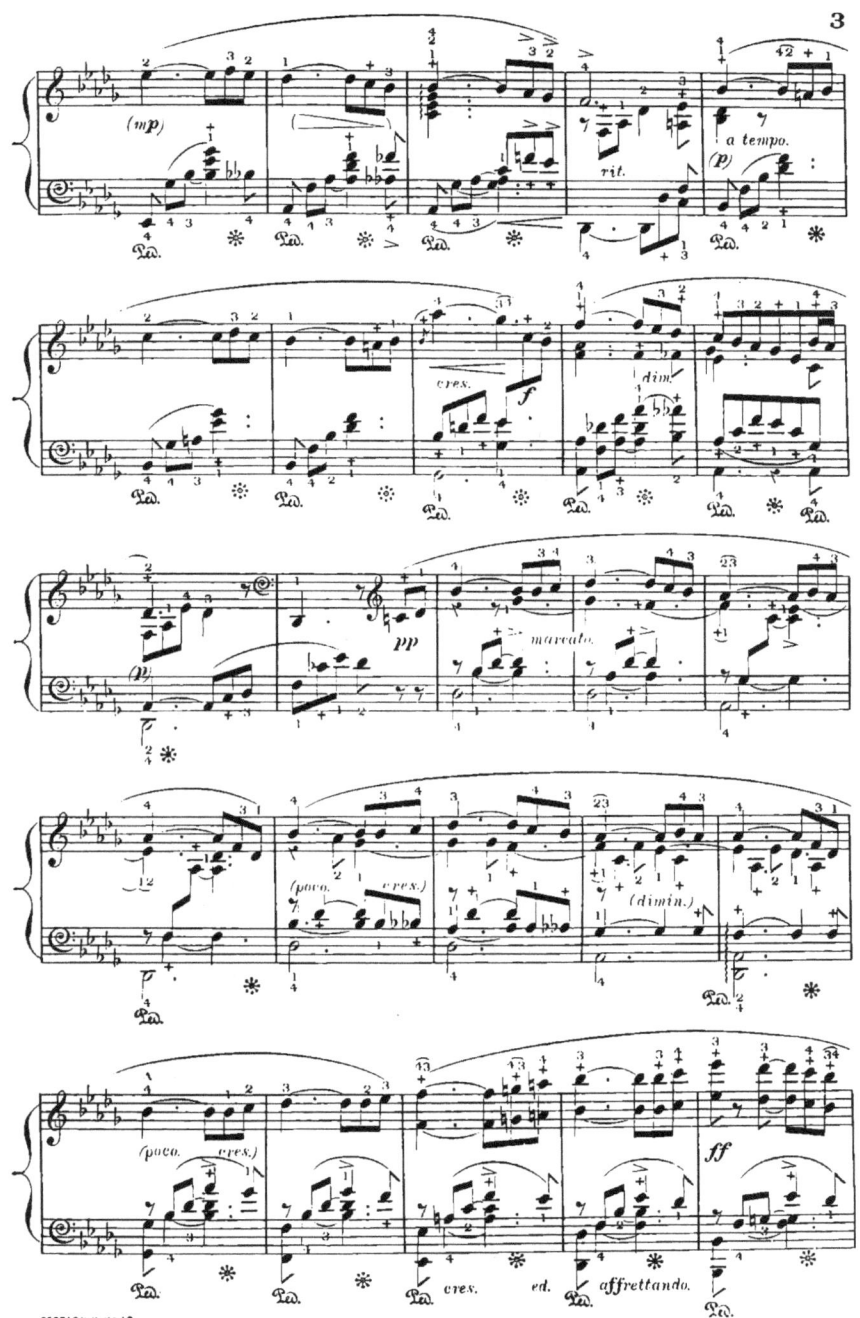

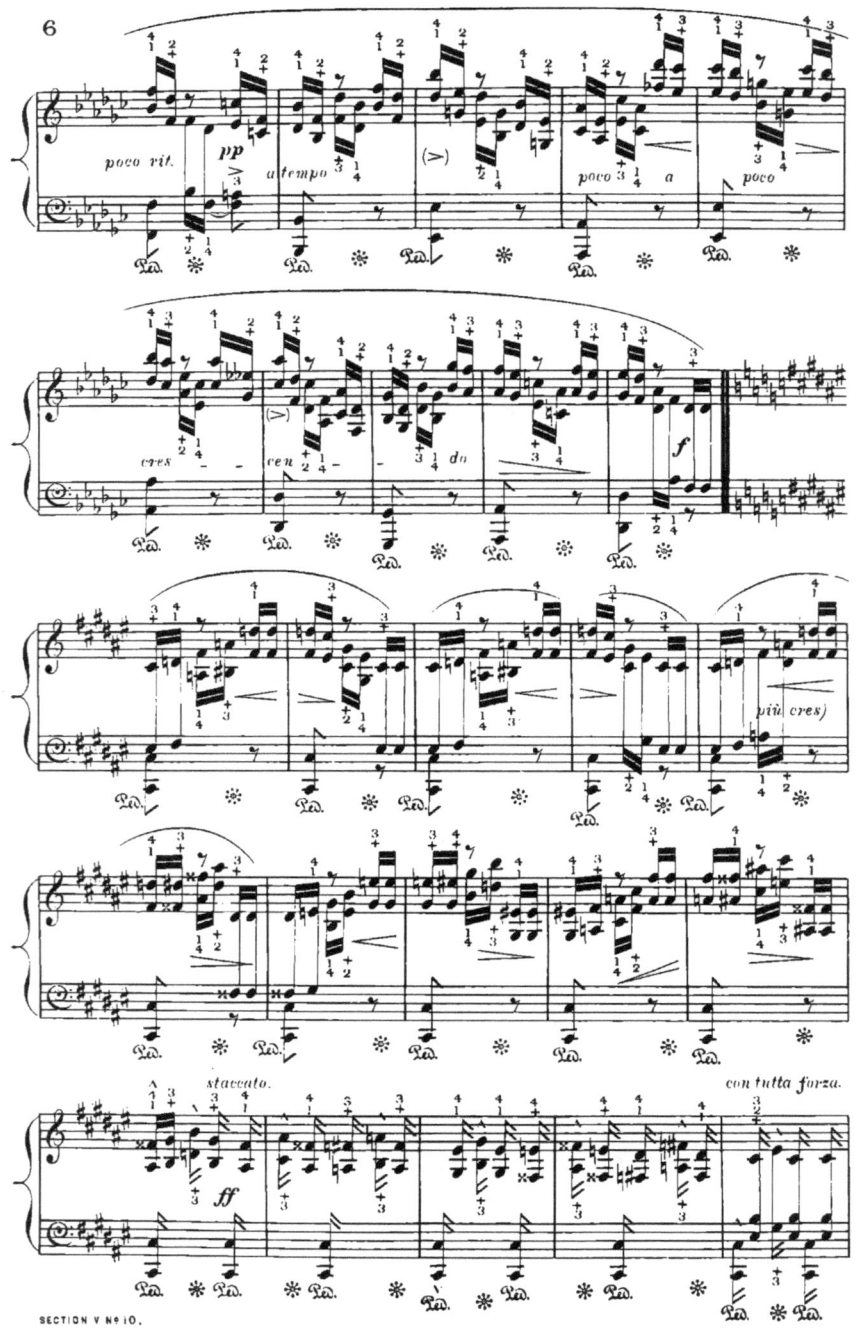

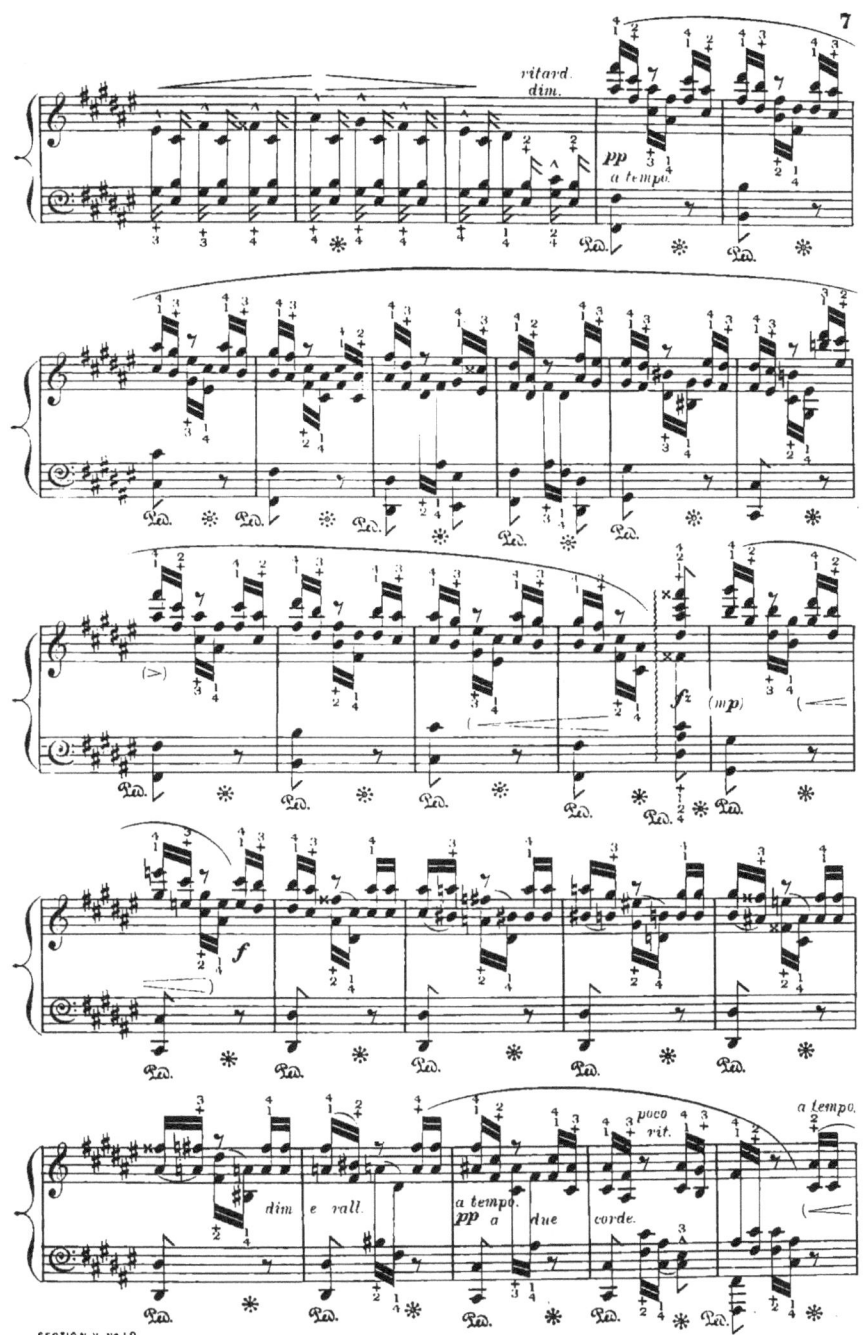

www.ingramcontent.com/pod-product-compliance
Lightning Source LLC
Chambersburg PA
CBHW031443160426
43195CB00010BB/832